Human Experience

SUNY series in Contemporary Continental Philosophy
Dennis J. Schmidt, editor

Human Experience

Philosophy, Neurosis,
and the Elements of Everyday Life

JOHN RUSSON

STATE UNIVERSITY OF NEW YORK PRESS

Published by
State University of New York Press, Albany

© 2003 State University of New York

For information, contact State University of New York Press, Albany, NY
www.sunypress.edu

Production by Kelli Williams
Marketing by Michael Campochiaro

Library of Congress Cataloging-in-Publication Data

Russon, John Edward, 1960-
   Human experience : philosophy, neurosis, and the elements of everyday life / John Russon.
     p. cm. – (SUNY series in contemporary continental philosophy)
   Includes bibliographical references and index.
   ISBN 0-7914-5753-2 (alk. paper) – ISBN 0-7914-5754-0 (pbk. : alk. paper)
     1. Phenomenological psychology. 2. Neuroses. I. Title. II. Series.

BF204.5.R87 2003
128'.4—dc21
                                                     2002044799

10 9 8

This work is dedicated to
Maria Talero,
a true friend
and a true philosopher.

We therefore must not recoil with childish aversion from the examination of the humbler animals. Every realm of nature is marvellous: and as Heraclitus, when the strangers who came to visit him found him warming himself at the furnace in the kitchen and hesitated to go in, is reported to have bidden them not to be afraid to enter, as even in that kitchen divinities were present, so we should venture on the study of every kind of animal without distaste; for each and all will reveal to us something natural and something beautiful. Absence of haphazard and conduciveness of everything to an end are to be found in nature's works in the highest degree, and the resultant end of her generations and combinations is a form of the beautiful.

—Aristotle, *Parts of Animals*, I.5.

Contents

Acknowledgments

This book draws on three main sources: growing up with a psychiatrist-father, a professional life devoted to the study of phenomenology, and many years' practice in private counseling. Whatever learning I have managed in this time has come through the help of many others, some of the most prominent of whom I would like to thank here. In no particular order I thank Irene Russon, Gordon Russon, E. B. Brownlie, Maria Talero, Eleanor Russon, Kym Maclaren, Pamela Lamb, Patricia Fagan, David Ciavatta, David Morris, Ed Casey, Luis Jacob, Bill Russon, Graeme Nicholson, Hugh Silverman, Tamar Japaridze, Charles Scott, James Morse, Robyn Parker, Susan Bredlau, Andrea Sauder, Anne Russon, Eugene Bertoldi, Celeste Superina, Art Krentz, Kirsten Swenson, George Marshall, Ellen Russon, Kenneth L. Schmitz, Kirsten Jacobson, Greg Recco, Jay Lampert, Evan Thompson, Len Lawlor, H. S. Harris, and the anonymous reviewers for the State University of New York Press. I am especially grateful to David Morris for sharing with me his thoughts on walking, which I have drawn on substantially in my discussion of this topic. I am also grateful to the Department of Philosophy at the Pennsylvania State University for support during the time of the writing of this book, and to my many students at Penn State, Acadia University and the University of Toronto.

Introduction

Contemporary European Philosophy has revolutionized the way in which we think about ourselves. Over the last two hundred years, such thinkers as Martin Heidegger, Sigmund Freud, Karl Marx, and Jean-Paul Sartre have challenged all of our most cherished and traditional views about what a person is and about what the world is. They have introduced powerful and compelling alternatives that have for the first time allowed us to resolve some of our longest-standing philosophical debates and have given us rich resources for solving the personal and social problems that plague our daily lives. These insights, however, are still only beginning to transform our ways of thinking and acting, are still only beginning to have a place in the shaping of our social institutions. It is my intention to contribute to this gradual process of transformation with this attempt at articulating the understanding of the human situation that has emerged from this two-hundred-year ferment.

Much of the progress of Contemporary European Philosophy has come from a focus on four specific themes: interpretation, embodiment, time, and the experience of others. It is this last theme, the theme of our relations with others, that affords the most exciting and immediately relevant insights into the human situation. The philosophical investigation into the nature of intersubjectivity has allowed us to understand the origins, structures and significance of the intimate relations between individuals, family life, the forms of political development, the deployment of power in society, and so on. It has been especially helpful in allowing us to understand and to deal with the problems we face in these contexts.

My intention is to articulate and defend what I understand to be the central thread of this view of the human situation, and to use it to bring into focus the psychological problems individuals face in trying to sort out their personal lives. It has often been claimed that philosophy is not relevant. I want to show instead how philosophy touches us precisely at those points in our lives where we face the greatest personal difficulty and where we are most in need of help. My goal is to show how the notion of the temporal, embodied, intersubjective self can allow us to understand the phenomena typically referred to as "mental illness." Specifically, I want to understand what neurosis is, I want to show why neurosis is a pervasive phenomenon in human life, and I want to develop the principles for dealing with ("treating") neurosis. What I intend to show is that mental health and the practice of philosophy are ultimately one and the same.

This is a book of philosophy as practiced in contemporary Europe, rather than a book about Contemporary European Philosophy. Its aim is the philosophical comprehension of the human situation according to the principles and teachings of the greatest thinkers of the past two hundred years. Consequently the reader will not find discussions of these thinkers in the following pages, but instead the use of their insights and investigations. Nonetheless, I want to say some orienting words about my position for the benefit of those readers who are already students of philosophy.

My study has primarily been guided by the insights of G. W. F. Hegel's *Phenomenology of Spirit* (1807), Martin Heidegger's *Being and Time* (1927), and Maurice Merleau-Ponty's *Phenomenology of Perception* (1945). It is with the work of these thinkers that I am primarily trying to establish a dialogue in this book. It is my view that these thinkers are more compatible with each other than incompatible, and my writing this work is in part an expression of my view that the study of Contemporary European Philosophy can sometimes be better served by synthetic attempts to think with the great philosophers than by intricate studies that seek to establish the finest points of difference.

From Hegel I have taken the idea that forms of experience inherently involve standards for their own evaluation, and that experiences transform themselves in light of these values. Throughout the book, I have tried to be guided by this notion of the inherent tension and dynamism within the different forms of human experience, and I have especially tried to connect it with a central notion that I take from Merleau-Ponty, namely, the way the body by its nature reaches beyond itself. I have tried to unite these two thoughts in my description of what I have called the "self-transcending" character of experience. From Hegel I have also taken the focus on the forms of interpersonal and social life, and the diagnosis of the central tensions and demands of these forms in terms of the notion of interpersonal recognition (*Anerkennung*). I have endeavored to link this with Heidegger's notion of *Mitsein*, that is, the way in which we are inherently "with" others, rather than being fundamentally "by ourselves." Also from Heidegger I have drawn my focus on the inherent temporality within experience, and upon the irreducibility of the "moody" character of our experience. I have tried to integrate these themes with Merleau-Ponty's focus on the intentionality of the body, and especially his emphasis on the way in which we live out of the habitual patterns we have developed for engaging with the world. In keeping with the practice of all three of these philosophers, I have defended the phenomenological method of analysis, that is, proceeding by way of the progressively more sophisticated description of the form in which experience is lived. Basically, I understand all three of these philosophers to have been led by phenomenological method to a very similar perception of the bodily and interpersonal character of our experience, and I find their various works to emphasize different, but compatible aspects of this perception.

My work is also substantially informed by another side of Contemporary European Philosophy that is most powerfully articulated in the works of Karl Marx, Sigmund Freud, and Gilles Deleuze and Felix Guattari. Each of these figures has produced intricate and compelling analyses of the primitive motors of experience, and each has emphasized (though in different ways) the bodily foundations of the developed meanings in our lives. In many ways, it is the analyses of desire, politics, and knowledge that these thinkers have produced that have most shaped my understanding of the specifics of human reality. Indeed, my own emphasis on mental illness (and its social and political context) is primarily inspired by these thinkers. These thinkers, however, do not provide the primary philosophical matrix for this work because of an orientation that they share, and that differs from an orientation shared by Hegel, Heidegger, and Merleau-Ponty. Marx, Freud, and Deleuze and Guattari all develop their analyses of the primitive motors of experience in such a fashion as to undermine the claims to autonomy made on behalf of the more developed forms of human experience, whereas Hegel, Heidegger, and Merleau-Ponty, while acknowledging the originariness of these primitive motors, also acknowledge the integrity of the emergent, "higher" forms of meaning. There is a fundamental way, in other words, that the philosophies of Marx, Freud, and Deleuze and Guattari, despite their profound insights into the dynamic and developing character of experience, are ultimately reductive in their understandings of the most definitive spheres of human experience. Therefore, while I have drawn substantially on the insights of these thinkers in this book, I also intend my argument to be a defense of the autonomy of the developed forms of human experience—of the "self," of "truth," and so on—and thus, in part, a challenge to what I see as the reductive tendency within this side of Contemporary European Philosophy.

I have also written this book with an eye to possible resonances with a number of other prominent figures within the history of philosophy. In particular, I have structured this work in response to Johann Gottlieb Fichte's *Fundamental Principles of the Entire Science of Knowledge* and René Descartes's *Meditations on First Philosophy*. My division of the work into three sections—"Form," "Substance," and "Process"—is intended as an allusion to Fichte's three fundamental principles (the ego positing itself, the ego opposing a not-self to itself, and the mutual limitation of finite self and finite other). In place of Fichte's self-positing ego, I propose the interpretive, temporal body as the first principle and absolute form of all meaning. My analysis of the way in which we exist as split into ourselves and our dealings with other people, and as split within ourselves in neurotic dissociation engages the domain of Fichte's second principle, the self's opposing of a not-self to itself, and identifies that with which we meaningfully contend in our lives, that is, the substance of human experience. Finally I offer the self-transformative practice of learning as the fundamental process of human experience, in place of Fichte's third principle of the mutual limitation of self and other as the dynamic ground of development and reconciliation within experience. In a similar fashion, I have written chapters 1 and 2 as a rough parallel to Descartes's first two meditations, in which he pioneered something like a phenomenological method, albeit inadequately. The substantial differences between my position and Descartes's demand that this study follow a divergent path after chapter 2, but the subsequent chapters are meant as a continuing rejoinder to Descartes, offering in comparison to his philosophy a new sense of the ego, a new sense of the body, and a new sense of rationality. In more subtle ways, I also intend the work to resonate with various works of ancient philosophy. One could think of my attempt to articulate the inherent dynamism within human life as a resurrection of something like Aristotle's notion of *phusis*, put to play, however, not within the realm of objective nature but within the realm of human experience; further, the section headings "Form," "Substance," and "Process" are intended to allude to progressively richer senses of Aristotle's notion of *ousia*, here the human *ousia*. Finally, my reference to the "elements" of everyday life is meant in loose parallel to Proclus' *Stoiceiosis Theologike*, such that this work might be thought of as, perhaps, a *Stoiceiosis Anthropologike*.

So, what will the reader find in the following pages? Part I, "The Form of Human Experience," lays out the fundamental principles for the adequate method of analyzing human experience. Chapter 1, "Interpretation," focuses on the way in which we are active in making sense of our experience, and on the notion that the way we make sense of things fundamentally draws on patterns of memory and expectation. Because the meaningfulness of what we experience is always shaped by our personal patterns of memory and expectation, human experience can only be understood by being approached "from the inside," so speak. Accordingly, chapter 1 also introduces the idea of a descriptive method for articulating the distinctive ways we have of making sense. Chapter 2, "Embodiment," further develops this idea of the patterns of memory and expectation that shape the sense of our experience, and argues that the patterns of memory and expectation have their own terms set primarily by our bodily capacities and by the kinds of significance to which they open us. All modes of experience are thus forms of bodily engagement with the world, and this chapter especially explores the idea that the body is a self-developing reality that, through processes of habituation, allows us to enter into ever more sophisticated ways of experiencing ourselves and our world. Chapter 3, "Memory," argues that the very form in which we experience objects is shaped by our habitual, bodily schemata of interpretation, and that, in particular, the identities of objects are in fact the repositories of our memories; this is true both of specific objects, which are meaningful to us in ways that resonate with our own specific past involvements, and of the world of objects as a whole, which we experience in our different moods as resonating as a whole with the orienting tone of our history as a whole. The shift of perspective on our own experience that was begun in chapter 1 with the introduction of the phenomenological method of description is thus shown, by the end of chapter 3, to result in a substantial shift of perspective regarding the nature of the objects of experience.

Part II, "The Substance of Human Experience," turns from the analysis of the way in which the human subject engages the world to considering what the human subject finds as the primary issues of concern in that world. Chapter 4, "Others," considers how the experiencing, bodily subject-engaged-in-a-world identified in chapters 1 to 3 naturally has dealings with other persons as the central concern within its experience, and explores the different types of social interaction that define the realm of human experience. The fundamental struggle that defines the life of the person is the pursuit of self-esteem and self-understanding, and this personal struggle is always contextualized by life in a family and life in a larger human society. Chapter 4 studies the different ways in which these different sectors of human experience—the personal, the familial, and the social—can both support and be in radical conflict with each other. Chapter 5, "Neurosis," brings together the different materials from the earlier chapters—interpretation, embodiment, memory, mood, and other people—to show how the tensions, demands, powers, and needs of the bodily subject are lived as a personality. In particular, this chapter focuses on the disparity between the ideal of "normalcy" that our social relations project, and the dissociative, compulsive, neurotic character into which a personality naturally develops. Chapter 5 ends with what is in many ways the "point" or the climax of the book, in a discussion of the bodily roots of the developed forms of human meaningful experience, and why these are naturally neurotic situations.

Part III, "The Process of Human Experience," addresses how the elements of human experience, identified in the preceding chapters point to the practice of conducting a human life. Chapter 6, "Philosophy," takes the findings of chapters 4, "Others," and 5, "Neurosis," on the substantial themes with which a human life is concerned, and addresses the way in which our lives are geared toward addressing the tensions and struggles that inherently emerge within personal and interpersonal life. This chapter focuses especially on the motivation toward self-transformation within human life, arguing that the shift of perspective initially introduced in chapters 1 to 3 is only fulfilled in processes of personal transformation by which we overcome crippling habits of self-interpretation. The conclusion of the book is that therapy, education, and philosophy are the proper arenas of human fulfillment, and this chapter tries to show how the analyses of human experience in Parts I and II offer the materials for such therapy.

Overall, my objective is threefold. First, I intend this work to be a contribution to the study of psychological health, of value both to those who study psychological health, and to those who are concerned about the health of their own psyches. Second, I intend this work to be a contribution to the study of Contemporary European Philosophy, of interest to those who specialize in the study of this area of philosophy and also to those who want to be introduced to this realm of thinking. Finally, it has been my intention to make a presentation of sufficient clarity and simplicity as to be substantially understandable by undergraduate students and educated adult readers with little or no background in philosophy. It is by the judgment of this last group of readers that I believe the real worth of this work will be measured.

Part I

The Form of Human Experience

1

Interpretation

Challenging Traditional Prejudices

What could be more obvious than that there is a world outside us and that we must make choices about how to deal with it? When we think about our place in the world, this is almost always what we imagine. Is it so obvious though? Is this the proper way to describe our situation? We can be a bit more precise.

When we reflect on ourselves, we typically start by recognizing ourselves as discrete agents facing a world about which we must make choices. The world is made up, it seems, of things with discrete identities that are present to us, right here, right now. On this familiar view, then, reality is a kind of aggregate, a bunch of distinct, separately existing things, one of which—me—faces those others and must self-consciously orchestrate her dealings with those things. These last few sentences, it seems to me, sum up the very core of almost all of our thinking experience of ourselves. Though quite simple, they nonetheless express the "theory" of reality with which we typically operate. The significance of these familiar views for our lives is immense. "And why not?" one might ask, since, "after all, those sentences describe how things really are, so they should be the foundation for everything we think." Indeed, this view seems so compelling as to be indubitable. It is, in fact, a standard way to mock philosophers to claim that they do doubt these ideas, wondering whether chairs exist, or whether they themselves really exist: these claims, in other words, seem so obvious that one would have to be a fool to entertain doubt about them.

Whether or not the philosophers should be mocked, it remains true that this cartoon of philosophical activity does in an important way describe the real work of philosophy. Indeed, it seems to me that the history of philosophy in general, and twentieth-century thought in particular, has taught us to be wary of the vision of the world described in my first sentences. As suggested above, the significance of these views is

9

indeed immense, but not because they are true. Rather, their significance comes from the extent to which our lives are crippled by too readily accepting this "theory" of things and of ourselves.

In the twentieth century, opposition to these views has come from many quarters. In recent years, ecologists have done a great deal to show us that our identities cannot be easily severed from the natural environments in which we live. Psychologists, for one hundred years at least, have investigated a wide range of experiences in which people do not seem to be free agents with full possession of the power of choice. Sociologists and anthropologists have shown how the way in which we see the world is largely reflective of cultural prejudices, so the identities of the objects we encounter are not clearly separable from our own social identities. All of these insights challenge the easy separation of subject and object upon which our familiar view is based.

[Probably the single most important aspect of the critique of this familiar view is found in the recognition that our experience is always interpretive: whatever perception we have of the world is shaped by our efforts to organize and integrate all of the dimensions of our experience into a coherent whole. How we go about this will be dictated by the level of our education, by our expectations, and by our desires, and so the vision we have will always be as much a reflection of ourselves and our prejudices as it is a discovery of "how things really are." In other words, the very way that we see things reveals secrets about us: what we see reveals what we are looking for, what we are interested in. This is as true of our vision of things that we take to be outside us as it is of our vision of ourselves.]

Focusing on the interpretive dimension to all experience allows us to shift away from the typical perspective we have upon ourselves on one side and the world on the other. We can now turn to our experience of the world and ask, "What do we reveal about ourselves through the way we experience?" or, "Who do we reveal ourselves to be by the way in which we see ourselves and our world?" When, for example, one of us experiences America as "home," this is not because there is some intrinsic property to America that makes it "homey." Rather, what we experience as the character of this object is fundamentally a reflection of our own expectations of security and ease of operation, based upon our memories of, and habituation to, this place. To others, of course, this same setting is threatening and oppressive. The homey or threatening character of this site is a reflection of our developed identities, and not of an inherent feature of the independent objects that confront us. Similarly, the experience of a woodland setting as a site for camping or as a site for logging reveals the interpretive perspective with which one engages with the world, rather than revealing the independent essence of the forest. This interpretive dimension, we shall see, is at play at every level of experience, from the most basic to the most developed forms of experience.

Shifting our focus to the interpretive dimension of experience opens up for us a new field of inquiry, a new object of study, namely, the field of our interpretive acts, the field of those acts through which we reveal the forms and limits of our powers of interpretation. Instead of accepting our immediate view of ourselves as obviously being discrete agents facing a world of present things about which we must make choices, we are now led to find our own identities to be a problem, a question. The same holds true for the things of the world. We are led to ask what the principles are behind the interpretive acts that give to us an integrated vision of ourselves and our world, who or what the agency is that enacts those interpretive principles, whether those principles are right, what consequences this structure of interpretation has, and so on. We are left, in short, with a task of discerning and evaluating the acts of interpretation that make our experience appear the way it does. We must, then, get clear on just how our experience does appear to us, with an eye to uncovering its founding acts of interpretation. I now want to give brief descriptions of some familiar experiences in order to show how interpretation is at play in our experience, and thereby to launch us into a new account of who we are and what our world is, that is, a new account of the relation of subject and object that is opposed to our familiar prejudices about ourselves and our world.

Interpretation, Synthesis, and Temporality

Think of what it is like to listen to music. Imagine a melody. Note that I say "a" melody: in an important sense the melody is single. It is certainly intrinsically varied, passing as it does through different pitches and rhythms, but what makes it a melody is that these differences are not separated one from the other. To hear a melody is precisely to retain the already sounded notes as a context against which the presently sounding note is being experienced, and to hear this note as equally anticipating further musical developments that will relate to the sound so far heard. To be a hearer of music, then, is at least to be able to entertain diversity within a single conscious act.

These diverse features of the music are not just lumped together like beans in a jar, either; rather, they are experienced as integrated, as mutually interpreting and contextualizing. The different notes do not just fall alongside each other, but are heard as working together in an organized fashion to allow the unity, the identity, of the music to express itself. To hear the music as music is to be able to hear how the multiplicity works together to achieve a unitary result. The experience of listening to music is well-described by Jean-Paul Sartre in his novel *Le Nausée*:

> At the moment, jazz is playing; there is no melody, just notes, a myriad of little quiverings. They don't know any rest, an inflexible order gives birth to them and destroys them, without even giving them the chance to recover, to exist for themselves. They run, they rush, they strike me in passing with a sharp blow, and they annihilate themselves. I'd really like to hold onto them, but I know that if I managed to stop one of them, there would be nothing left between my fingers but a roguish, languid sound. I must accept their death, indeed I must *will* it. (p. 36, my translation)

As this example makes clear, listening to music is an experience built out of the relations between and among the notes, and it is an active experience in the sense that it requires a well-prepared and engaged listener. The notes of a jazz tune fly past, and in so doing they carve out a space that one can inhabit with one's imagination in concentrated attention or with one's swinging body in dance. But this musical reality cannot be frozen and grasped—it only exists in its temporal passing. A particular note, so exciting or moving when heard at the climax of some passage in the song, has none if its force if separated out and heard in isolation. The other notes that contextualize the note we are now hearing are both past and future, and these temporal determinations are not contingent features, but are definitive formal features of the music, that is, the temporal order is essential: to play the same notes in a different order would be to play a different piece of music. Music, then, only exists for a being that can "tell time," so to speak. The music can only be heard by one who attends to the music in the integrity of its flow, who hears the sense of the music passed on from one note to the next. The listener must come to inhabit the music, join with it in anticipating its further development, and hear the notes that present themselves in the context of what has already sounded. Sometimes we cannot hear this integration and sense within the sounds, when we hear styles of music with which we are not familiar, and it can take a great deal of time and effort on our part to "develop an ear" for such music. It is only when we have developed this ability to hear how the various parts work together that we really consider ourselves to be hearing the music. It is only because we can be thus "musical" that there can be music for us. Such musicality is a form of our general ability to comprehend the integration or unitary sense of a temporally extended, experiential diversity.

[This power to comprehend an inherently temporal, varied, single experience we can call (following the practice of Immanuel Kant in his *Critique of Pure Reason*), "synthesis," meaning the ability to recognize things in their togetherness. The particular synthetic power of maintaining as definitive of the present that which is not in itself present (i.e., in our example, the past and future music), has traditionally been called "imagination," that is, the ability to entertain in consciousness that which is not currently present. Such imaginative synthesis is the precondition, the *conditio sine qua non*, of our experience of temporally meaningful, intrinsically varied unities. This means, in fact, that such imaginative synthesis is the condition of our experience *simpliciter*, for all experiences are temporal and intrinsically varied: all our experiences carry on something like this melodic, harmonic, and rhythmic flow whereby one moment seems to grow out of the last and to melt into the next in a way that "keeps the tune going," so to speak, while developing it into a new richness.]

Typically, when we think of imagination we think of fantasizing or engaging in some kind of fanciful and self-conscious extrapolation beyond what is real. In referring to imagination here, however, we must not think simply of what we explicitly do when we daydream. Rather, the imagining under consideration here is an activity we never do without. To feel in some situation that we have "arrived" is to experience that moment in light of the context set up by what preceded it: the present is here experienced in light of the no-longer-present. Again, a sudden feeling of fear or comfort in some setting is the experience of that present in light of what is not-yet-present, what threatens. We can also imagine countless examples of richer ways in which our daily experience evinces a harmonic and rhythmic flow that allows the experience of a certain melodic unity, a certain sense. A conversation with a colleague over dinner, the passing of the workday, the recognition of my friend's familiar footsteps on the stairs, the ability to drive a car—steer, accelerate, shift gears, turn off the windshield wipers, watch the road, read the signs, listen to the radio, smoke, talk with my passenger, stop and go with the traffic light—these are so many synthetic experiences, experiences dependent on our power of imagination, integrated experiences of a unified sense being manifested through a complex and temporally varied diversity. That power we are familiar with in our self-conscious daydreaming is rather a luxurious use of this most basic power we have to hold to-gether—to synthesize—what is present with what is not present, the power that underlies all of our experience. As experiencers, then, we simply are synthetic processes of imaginative interpretation.

Just as we can be misled by the term *imagination*, so can we be simi-larly misled by the description of our experience as interpretive or syn-thetic. Typically, we think of interpretation as an activity we perform upon an already acquired object, and synthesis, similarly might typically suggest binding together two pieces that are already present. This typical model of an action performed upon an already acquired material is not, however, the proper model for understanding the interpretive character of experience. Experience is not a two-stage process in which we first get data and then construct an interpretation. On the contrary, it is only as already shaped by our interpretive orientation that our experience ever begins. In other words, the way we immediately notice the new moments of our experience is always in terms of the meaningful contexts we have already been developing. This point will be clearer if we consider an-other experience.

When I hear a language spoken that is foreign to me, I hear sounds—perhaps a kind of "music." This is the only level on which the speaker's speaking impinges on me meaningfully. This, however, is not the experi-ence of others who might be around me who understand the language: those who know the language would react in a way that I could neither predict nor explain—indeed, if I did not know intellectually what was happening, the situation would appear more as a kind of magical conjur-ing than as communication, with the sounds being sent out in the hope of creating some response. The only way I could come to understand this language would be to engage in an elaborate process of language study, which would eventually involve listening to these sounds and constructing an interpretation. This process of language study, then, is an experience that does involve a two-step process of data collection and interpretation. What is noteworthy about this is that it is an uncommon or extraordi-nary approach to language: this is not the way we usually experience hearing language spoken.

To hear a foreign language is to hear uninterpretable music with magical effects. When I hear someone speak my own language, however, everything changes. Rather than "conjuring," one who speaks my language seems to be handing me meanings directly. I do not have to establish what words the sounds represent and then struggle to decide what story these words tell. On the contrary, in normal circumstances the other's meaning is immediately available to me. In fact, in listening to speech, I usually do not hear "sounds" at all, but am offered instead an intelligible world. Indeed, the "raw sounds" of my own language are for me a kind of aural "blind spot." I cannot really hear the "music" of the sounds of my own language: I do not know what my language "sounds like" in the way that I can recognize the typical sounds of a foreign language. Indeed, far from having to make sense of sounds that I hear, the meaningfulness of my language holds me in a context where I have no option besides hearing the meanings. In other words, I am not capable of not understanding what meanings are being presented when I hear another speaking.

We here notice the basic form taken by our imaginative interpretation. Only in hearing a foreign language, that is, a language that does not live for us, do we hear sounds that suggest to us a problem for interpretation. When I hear my own living language, this stage of reflective interpretation does not happen at all, and it is this experience that reveals the form that interpretation fundamentally takes in our experience. The interpretation that constitutes experience is not a two-stage act of first receiving an uninterpreted object and then overlaying it with an interpretation; rather, it is only as already interpreted that there is for me a phenomenon. There are no raw data awaiting organization by a subsequent act. In experience, I directly perceive the object as a unitary, already meaningful phenomenon. Only subsequently can the different elements be separated out from their initial "melodic" presentation through an act of reflective consideration. They are not experienced prior to, and external to, the unified phenomenon. The interpretive character of our experience, in other words, is our distinctive way of originally being open to something making sense to us at all: interpretation does not have a raw material, but is how we first become open to having any "material" at all. Indeed, whatever would count as "material" would already need to be acknowledged by us as a recognizable unity, and this recognition of unity would already involve activities of interpretive synthesis.

Let us carry further this account of how the interpretive experience is given as already unified. I have already mentioned the place of anticipation in the experience of the presence of the melody. I want to work toward taking up this temporal dimension more carefully by first considering experiential phenomena in terms of their "expressive" capacity. In particular, I want to describe how the objects of our experience lead us down paths of expectation in a way that we experience as compelling: we experience objects as demanding of us that we develop our situation toward a specific future.

In our day-to-day dealings we rely heavily upon habits we have developed for coping with the most familiar situations. It may be the case that each morning we go through the same routine for making coffee, or that we drive the same route to get to work. Sometimes we deliberately set out to change our routine. This is not always easy, however. Sometimes we launch ourselves down a new path and we find unexpectedly that our habits have taken over and that we have done the usual thing rather than carrying out the atypical action we had intended. Perhaps I began making coffee when I did not want to, or I found myself driving to work when I meant to go somewhere else. In such experiences, our habitual ways of behaving show themselves to be more powerful than our explicit reflective decisions.

What these experiences reveal is that the familiar objects of our world have a kind of momentum within experience that can shape our behavior. This shows the inadequacy of our typical assumption that objects exist in a state of independence and indifference to us, and that they are easily subjected to our choices. The experiences of unintentionally making coffee and unintentionally driving to work show that I do not encounter my kitchen utensils as indifferent disconnected objects that I subsequently decide how to use, nor do I encounter indifferent spatial locations in relation to which I decide my path. On the contrary, I experience interpretively charged environments, things, and places that carry within them a directive force. Just as we saw in the experience of hearing my native language, here too what I experience are environments that already have meanings embedded in them, and the kinds of meanings they have are essentially directional, that is, they direct my actions toward some end. The coffeepot bears within it its connection to other things and to me, and it simply means "plug me in"; the intersection at the end of the block means "go left." It is as thus making these demands upon me that I immediately experience these objects. The phenomena of my world are fundamentally expressive, and they express themselves in the form of demands, of calls to action. They present themselves as expectant, pregnant with anticipated fulfillment, and express a call to me to complete them, to satisfy them, to be the deliverance of their latent significance. Objects are not indifferent and alien, and they do not passively receive our explicit choices. They draw us forward like magnets, without our self-conscious control.

[Contrary to our traditional assumptions, then, this is the form that experience typically takes: we are imaginative, interpretive, synthetic subjects for whom objects are meaningful calls to action that direct our life without our self-conscious intervention. Objects as they figure within our experience are not discrete and alien, but, like notes in a melody, they are embedded in contexts with other objects with which they mutually interpenetrate, and they *already* penetrate and impinge upon us. We, in turn, find ourselves already committed to various situations such that we find our choices made for us, rather than being self-contained choosers who stand aloof from things.]

Notice that this description, by showing that we are not the alienated, autonomous choosers we typically take ourselves to be, also shows that our familiar assumption that we can easily know ourselves through simple introspection is mistaken. We cannot immediately know ourselves through simple introspection, because the view that introspection gives is the very view we have just criticized. Self-knowledge, that is, does not come through the easy reflection upon ourselves that we typically rely upon, but, on the contrary, will only come through a study of the determinate forms of interpretive synthesis that can be discerned within the character of objective calls to action ("objective" in the sense of, "pertaining to the nature of the object"): the terms in which we experience the object as calling upon us reflect the values and projects through which we experience the world. Our preliminary results have shown that such a study of the implicit significance of the forms of our objects, by revealing the temporal, synthetic character of experience, will be a critique of the familiar view of the self as immediately present to itself as a chooser amid present, discrete objects.

Our talk of interpretation could be recast to say that it is our prejudices that are reflected in the way we experience the world. Our study so far was itself already designed to challenge some of our most basic prejudices. Perhaps the general prejudice that most informs our experience, and of which the various prejudices we studied are species, could be called the prejudice of "presence." We typically treat reality as if the truth of things is in their immediate presence, and as if it is by being immediately present to something that we get its truth. Thus we take ourselves to be able to be immediately present to ourselves through introspection, we take things to be present to us as objects confronting our perception, we trust the "reporter" who was "present" at the event over the "interpreter" who appraises the event by evidence collected by others, we treat things as if their reality is present in them and in them alone, and so on. Our study of the synthetic, temporal, interpretive form of experience has already shown us how this privileging of presence is a significant misrepresentation, inasmuch as the subject is not immediately present to introspection, neither the object nor the subject holds its identity simply present within itself alone, and all experience is inherently mediated by interpretation and time.

Our description of the basic form that experience takes has begun to show us the inadequacies of the prejudice in favor of presence, and this critique can be developed further. Rather than recognizing presence as the ultimate ground of reality, the full-fledged description of experience—the philosophical approach called "phenomenology"—would show *negativity, difference, deferral, absence, distance, ambiguity, duplicity,* and *concealment* to be the primary terms in which the motor and substance of our world is to be articulated rather than simply the *positivity, self-sameness, immediacy, presence, proximity, clarity, univocity,* and *obviousness* that our prejudice insists on. Rather than looking to some supposedly independent object in order to find out its intrinsic sense, phenomenology will consider how it is that the objects of our experience are meaningful only in light of their contextualization within the structures of memory and expectation that define a particular perspective. We can begin to see this inversion of traditional values if we look once more at the experience of listening to a melody.

The melody is only present to us through the differing of the notes, and the notes themselves are present only insofar as they point behind themselves, reinvoking the absent, contextualizing past, and point ahead of themselves, deferring the fullness of the musical moment to the controlling power of the notes yet to come: the presence of the melody is precisely how the notes differ. What we naively take to be "hearing a note" is thus truly a hearing of what the single note is not. And, indeed, more than just the notes not-being each other, it is our own not-being the melody itself—being aware of it precisely by not simply being identical with it, not being utterly absorbed in it, but still reserving the distance that is "being aware of"—that lets the melody be. "There is" a note, then, only insofar as it is an arrangement of negations, both the ordered negation of the contextualizing notes that precede it, succeed it, and harmonize it, and the negation of the one for whom there is a melody. To hear a melody is precisely to hear what is realized through these "is nots."

These two sides of "the negative"—the absence that is past and future and the distance that is the awareness—are in truth the same. The past is how the awareness still holds on to that which has been and the future is how the awareness already holds on to that which will be. This is what we first recognized in referring to experience as a temporal synthesis: it is as retaining and expecting that one is able to be aware of (by being distant from) a present. It is this temporal character of experience that is the "negativity" that lets there be presence. It is by our existing as temporalizing—as engaging past, present, and future together—that there is a present. (The very concept of the present itself points to this conclusion: "now" only is to the extent that it is not "then," that is, now brings into relief *now* what is not now, and thus the very premise of presence itself is that there is presence only because it makes present what is not present.) The very nature of our subjectivity, then, is to be "simultaneously" in the past, the present, and the future. Just as our object is never a simple present but is constituted by negation and absence, so are we never fully present, never simply here, but instead we are always outside of ourselves, somewhere other than where we are. It is by being retaining and expecting that we can be present—that there can be something present to us—and it will thus be by understanding our processes of retention and expectation that we will come to understand who we are and what our world is. It is our memories and our goals that are condensed into the presentation—the appearing—that is experience. How things are present, then, is the revelation of our projects and our memories. It is indeed in the present that we will find out who we are, but only after we have abandoned the prejudice of the primacy of presence.

We must, then, turn to what is presented—turn to the appearing that is experience—and let it show us who we are. This approach to the description of consciousness that is not prejudiced in favor of the present entails that we must let ourselves be guided by *how* the present presents itself, and allow its movement to reveal to us who it is who is experiencing, rather than beginning with views taken from our familiar vision of things and insisting that these be used to explain what is experienced.

Description, Happening, and Situation

If we free ourselves of the traditional prejudices about the subject and the object as fully present and mutually alien entities between which a relation has to be created, what our description of experience reveals instead is that the relation itself comes first, that is, it is from the primary relation—the act of experiencing—that subject and object come to be established, and not vice versa. What is first is a situation of experience in which all of the participants—subjects and objects—are already shaped and defined by the others. The subject and the object are not indifferent beings that might or might not come into relation: they are already involved, each having a grip on the other. How the object exists is reflective of the interpretive demands of the subject; equally, the subject is already subordinated to the demands of the object. In other words, each taken by itself is an abstraction, something that can only be separated in reflective thought and not in reality. We must, therefore, reorient our thinking and conceive of a subject who is intrinsically situated, or an environment that intrinsically calls for someone to resolve it. What exists is a situation that is meaningful, a situation that is experienced as a range of tensions, a situation that needs certain things to be done. Human reality is this situation, this event of meaning, this happening of a subject-object pair.

In identifying the subject-object pair as the human reality, we have gone beyond any appeal either to a more original choosing agent that goes out to meet an alien object, or to an objective truth that forces itself onto an alien subject for explaining why things are the way that they are. This is because we have seen that the subject and the object so conceived only exist as abstracted aspects of the meaningful situation, the comprehending relation. This entails that there is nothing beyond this meaningful situation to which one could turn to justify, explain, test, or prove the significance of human reality. Consequently, it is what occurs as the situation of human meaning that must be the ground, guide, and measure of all our investigations and self-interpretations. In order to know, then, we will rely on the authority neither of the scientist nor the theologian. Knowledge will ultimately be a matter of describing what happens, and this description of the form experience takes will be the last word.

We have begun such a description of the form of the human situation in this chapter. We have seen the decisive roles of remembering and projecting in shaping this situation. In chapter 2 we will see that this story of the remembering projector who is the intertwining of subject and object is the story of the body-subject that forms habits.

2

Embodiment

The Body as Touching-Touched

People can hurt us. A woman alone at night can be grabbed by a man on the street; she can be beaten and raped and left paralyzed or pregnant or syphilitic. A police officer can use the threat of hurting that is implied by his gun and uniform to get an innocent and intimidated black man to bow and grovel. A boy can be sodomized by his father every day for years without having any capacity to challenge or escape this invasion. A mother can slap or spank her child when the child cries in distress. Indeed, that we live in this structure of being open to the invasions of stronger others is one of our earliest discoveries.

We have other early discoveries, of course. Freud argues that we first experience the world through the mouth: the child at the breast experiences making a connection that lets a flow start and discovers that warm, wet, and tasty happens. In such early experiences we discover that we are open to pleasure. Over the course of our development, our pleasure-seeking grows more complex, especially in that we become more active in our pursuits. This development of activity and complexity in our pursuit of pleasure is equally the development by which we come to have a progressively more sophisticated sense of ourselves and of our world.

Both of these structures, being open to being hurt and being open to the pursuit of pleasure, are structures of embodiment. It is as bodies that we can be invaded, and it is as bodies that we can act in the world. It is as embodied that we can touch and be touched. Our bodies are the determinateness, the specificity, of our existence: the body is the point where each of us is something specific. To be a body is to be a specific identity that is open to involvement with others. Indeed, pleasure and pain are the two faces of this involvement, the ways in which that with which we are involved either welcomes or hinders our determinacy. Our bodies are the living processes by which we establish contact with reality.

By being the point of contact of ourselves and our world, our embodiment is also our being public: it is as bodies that we are visible, tangible, and tasteable by others. Our embodiment is where we show ourselves, where our specificity is open to the judgment of others. The vulnerability to the violent ingress of the armed attacker that is characteristic of the body is mirrored by the psychological vulnerability that comes with our being on public display. The body is the point of intersubjective contact: the point where who we are cannot be concealed and cannot be held to be a matter of private interpretation, the site of shame and pride, of intimidation and seduction.

Trespass, pleasure, shame, seduction: these and other such terms are the ones that name the terrain of embodiment. Fundamentally, the body *is* our participation in these realities. These terms identify the logical components that are definitive of embodiment, and it is in these terms that the body must be understood. These terms—trespass, pleasure, shame, and seduction—name ways that we in our very identities are sensitive to what is outside us. Being sensitive—being the possibility for experience—is the essence of the body. We are beings who are sensitive to our environments; we care about how we stand with others, and our relations with others affect us—we feel our placement within the world. These feelings take place at many levels: we can be affected at a very immediate and superficial level by the shape and texture of some mass or at a very intimate level by how another's sense of our worth touches our self-estimation. These layers of relation—these feelings—are the way the body exists. To be a body is to be open to noticing how we stand with others—to have others already influencing, already inside our experience. By virtue of being bodies, how we stand with others matters to us, which means that it is as a bodily involvement with another that we are invaded, that we are satisfied, that we are embarrassed, and that we enchant. This involvement is the experience of being engaged with others, of already being open to their influence and being able to influence them. As bodies, we are in touch with others in the richest and fullest sense of being "in touch with." The body is our experience of "contact."

This conception of embodiment, however, is very much at odds with the terms we typically deploy to take account of bodies. In our culture we have developed the reflex of thinking in terms of mass, extension, viscosity, and similar notions when we think of bodies. Such concepts treat the body as inert and passive, as "raw material," as an object rather than a subject, and they thus assume a fundamental separation between the body and experience, as if "to experience" were one thing and "to be a body" something separate and unrelated. This familiar way of thinking, however, shuts us off from comprehending the phenomena of human embodiment, which is the very matrix of all of our experience, all of our engagement with significance. This familiar attitude toward the body, which treats the body as just an indifferent material object within experience rather than its source, is of a piece with the prejudice of presence and the prejudice of discrete selfhood that we considered in chapter 1. If we rely on these concepts that reduce the body to "material," we shall never be able, for example, to understand such experiences as shame or erotic attraction. Let us consider further this central prejudice about embodiment.

Our typical starting point for thinking about bodies is to contrast them with minds. Minds, we say, think, and thoughts have no mass, no spatial expanse, no materiality. Bodies, we say, occupy space, and can be measured and observed. Minds and bodies, we say, are two fundamentally different kinds of things. This division between intelligence and spatial massiveness is quite pervasive in our day-to-day discourse but it is ultimately logically incoherent and untenable as a view of reality. We can see the problems to which this view gives rise if we consider what the relation of such a separated mind and body would be like in the living human being. We will see, in fact, that our familiar way of thinking of mind and body actually rests on a conceptual absurdity.

We typically presume the mind and the body to be really radically different kinds of things, such that minds engage solely with mental processes and bodies solely with bodily processes. If this is so, then they can have no feature in common, no common ground, for all of the features of the body will necessarily be bodily, and all of the features of the mind will be mental, and there can be no shared feature of each that is somehow both bodily and mental for the very premise here is that if a feature is one of these (bodily or mental) it cannot be the other. If they have nothing in common, they can have no point of contact, because the point of contact itself would have to be a shared feature, would have to be of a piece with both mental "stuff" and bodily "stuff." But this is precisely what the dualistic hypothesis denies: if being mental and being bodily are radically different there cannot be some reality in which they are identical. Thus, if they are radically different in their being, and can therefore have no common point of contact, it follows that there can be no relationship between the mind and the body, that they must permanently remain radically alien in all aspects of their existence. If this is true, however, it is clear that this way that we typically describe minds and bodies cannot possibly apply to the existence of human beings, for it is precisely the relationship of the mind and the body that is definitive of our experience and that needs to be explained.

Even if we were to accept the radical separation of mind and body, we would still have to acknowledge that what seems definitive of the human body is that it is responsive to the human mind. I am typing at this moment. The typing reflects my desire to type and expresses my thoughts, my mind, the me that is my identity. The typing, however, is an action of my body: it is because of my thoughts and desires that my body types. This implies that my mental life is indeed related to my bodily life, and it is related in the especially strong way that is a causal relationship. Similarly, pumping various bodies into my body—caffeine, alcohol, and heroin—dramatically affects my perception; once again, my body and my mind are related, again in a causal fashion. What has to be explained, in other words, is how it can be the case that the state of my experience is *because of* the state of my body and that the state of my body is *because of* the state of my experience.

We can see this even more strikingly when we consider the simple example of touching. It is I who touches things, I, the thinking, feeling mind; but it is equally my body that touches things, that feels. In sex, it is I who am sensitive to the touch of another, and it is only because it is I who am touched that I care about sex: I want my partner to touch me. What touches and is touched, what is sensitive, is the very thing that forms my identity, and this my identity is clearly my body. When we describe the actual experience of the living human being who touches and is touched, we really cannot even talk of a "relation" of mind and body, for in this experience these two are undifferentiatable. Similarly, what types—the one and only thing that types, and that is one and the same with itself—is equally and simultaneously identifiable as my mind and my body. Again, it is equally my mind and my body—me—that is drugged.

Like our familiar views about the discrete self-containedness of our own existence (our mind) and about the primacy of presence in general, our familiar views about the mind and the body offer a way of thinking about things that cannot actually map onto our experience. Indeed, what a description that is truthful to our actual experience reveals is that there is only one "thing" at play in our experience and that is "I" and this "I" is a body that thinks, feels, and touches. I am a thinking body, a feeling body, a touching body: I am the very thing that cannot possibly be comprehended by the system of interpretive categories that begins by radically dualizing mind and body. In place of these inadequate categories, then, we need the concept of a body as a sensitive thing, of a body as cognizant.

This idea does certainly demand that many of our familiar ways of thinking about things change. At the same time, though, there are a number of ways in which we are already familiar with this approach to thinking of bodies as cognitive. When we think of the body's immune system, for example, we think of an intelligent, bodily agency that recognizes and is responsive to the dynamic changes within its environment. Similarly, we often think of plants—to which we do not attribute anything like an explicit consciousness or self-consciousness—as behaving, that is, as responding in a discriminating way to changes within their environments. Though we would not think of these bodies as self-conscious, as "minds," we do, in these cases, think of bodies that are able to recognize, respond, and behave with discrimination: these are behaviors that express primitive levels of rationality and initiative, the two powers we typically reserve for minds. These are not robot bodies pushed by some other intelligent being. The body that is a white blood cell is itself an intelligent body, a body that in its very being discriminates meaningfully between intelligible features within its environment. The plant similarly has no one to direct it, but acts on its own, intelligently. These bodies are not led by some other self-conscious being, nor are they themselves explicitly self-conscious. On the contrary, what each of these bodies reveals is that the mind is not another thing separate from the body, but that the body is that which acts intelligently, that which is itself an intelligent responsiveness to its environment. It is along the lines of our typical understanding of these natural phenomena that we must reorient our thinking about human minds and bodies.

The body is living, material discrimination. There is not some other subject "behind" the body that is choosing for it and propelling it into action. Its object, furthermore, is not some causal "thing-in-itself" that is forcing the body to respond in certain ways. Rather, instrinsic to the body is its own immanent sensitivity, its own perspective, and initiative, its own desires, and the object to which it responds is an object *already interpreted in terms of* the norms and concerns projected by the body itself. The body responds meaningfully to an object that itself is meaningful to the body in light of that body's own orientation. The body is inherently "knowing," then, in that in its behavior it discrimates meaningfully between aspects of its object, and its object is itself shaped by the norms projected by the body; it is the body's "environment." To be embodied is to be engaged in a behavioral knowing of an environment, and this performance of knowing is definitive of the identities of the knowing agent and the object known. We, as living bodies, are dynamic processes of establishing contact, of getting in touch. It is in this process, through this process, and as this process that both what is contacted and who contacts come into being. This contact itself, this living, material discrimination, is the very substance of our existence.

Between two spatial areas the boundary is at one and the same time the end of one area and the beginning of the next, and in an analogous way bodily contact is no more subject than object. In contact there is a dynamic tension of two opposed poles—the subject and the object—that define themselves against each other while simultaneously implicating each other in themselves. As we should expect from our studies in chapter 1, if we are to understand the human body, we must abandon our familiar conception of a fully constituted self and fully constituted other that exist on their own as independent realities, just as we must abandon the dualism of mind and body. Instead, we must come to understand existence as simply the dynamic of embodiment within which the two poles of self and other come to be defined, and out of which the substance of their development into complex self-identities grows. Embodiment and experiencing are thus inseparable, for it is how we are bodies that determines how there can be others for us.

Our body itself offers us a first sketch of reality. Reality, it announces, is what answers to the determinatenesses that are my hands, my mouth, my height, and so on. In other words, each way in which my body is figured offers the possibility of a distinctive form of contact, and thus offers the first "categories" by which what is can be comprehended. For the child, the world first appears as what can be tasted and sucked, what can please or displease my skin, my sense of balance, my sense of warmth, what is soft, pliant, or resistant under my hands; it is the comfortable and welcoming softness I lie upon, but also the hard and slippery obstacle I must traverse to obtain that softness. For us, our body is not initially an object to be comprehended or a system under our control, but is a multiplicity of openings, of revelations, of connections that let various flows start, a multiplicity that offers determinations for our interest—for our pleasure, pain, or whatever more sophisticated concerns we have—and that also places demands upon us. It is the gradual elaboration of these figured openings that is the emergence of the distinct and complex identities of subject and object.

Because the form of all embodiment is contact, all the figured openings of the living body, of the sketch, are splittings: the openings take the form of interpenetrations of what could be analyzed into a subject contacting and an object contacted, though this duality need not be thematized within the contact itself. Each figured contact, then, implies an experiential structure of "there is . . ." "for. . . ." "Being for a subject," or "having an object" is thus the generic form of bodily contact. To be a body-subject, in other words, means to have an object, which means to have an other. It is thus also the very nature of embodiment to be a putting of itself into publicity, that is, it is a defining of a subject for which there is also already defined another point of view—an outside. Embodiment is the splitting into inside and outside, into my point of view and a point of view on me. To be a body, then, is to be already defined with reference to other vantage points: each point of figured contact defines something else for which the body has an outside. The body touches, contacts others, only because it is itself touched by those others.

The initial forms that these figurings take are defined by the given form of our bodily organism: how we are embodied determines the shape of our initial sketch. The actions we engage in, though—the actions that elaborate the initial openings—make more determinate and more complex the identities of the potential subject and object of each contact. Let us consider the process that is the developing of more complex relationships, which means the developing of more complex identities for the subject and the object.

Habituation

The body does not begin as an instrument under the explicit control of a discrete, self-conscious agent, but is, rather, the very medium of existence within which such an agency can emerge. The body begins as the loosely organized arrangements of contacts. Each of these contacts exists as a "there is . . . for, ..." that is, each defines a specific relationship that is an object for a subject—the "splitting" referred to above. For each of these determinate relatings of specific object to specific subject, the body provides the contextualizing ground, the basic figuring of the sketch. In other words, the form in which the object is made available and the form in which the subject is interested are both given by the form of the bodily contact itself. Now these contacts themselves are so many local points of contact that have the further character of aiming beyond themselves. They aim, however, without an overarching map provided for a greater terrain than themselves. This aiming is what we next need to consider.

Consider, for example, the hand. Its character is "to grasp," which means always to be open to reach beyond its immediacy to something else not contained in itself. The same is true of the "to touch" of our flesh or the "to taste" of our tongue: in each case, the organs take us to "beyond." The very way these contacts give an object, a "beyond," is as something that has the possibility of being developed further: the "beyond" that they reach is not exhausted in the touch, but is a site for continuing exploration and enhanced perception. This further development is not itself a "content" that is explicitly given with the object, but is a range of possible development that must be made actual by further bodily activity. My body, for example, discovers a floor beyond itself, which itself invites further crawling to locations "beyond" that are only discoverable through further bodily contact. (Indeed, the very realization that there should be an overarching map in which the entire content of reality is already discovered and given in advance is itself one of the—rather sophisticated, and also problematic—developments of the initial contacts: it is through the gradual development of bodily contact that we come to develop a notion of "reality itself" or being-as-a-whole. This notion is itself complex, and our thoughts about this "reality as such" are typically subject to analogous prejudices to those we have already been diagnosing.) Thus, while the contacts themselves are determinate (i.e., each defines itself as a differential relation of a determinate object for a determinate subject), they are determinatenesses that point beyond themselves to the possibility (and, indeed, at certain levels of development, to the demand, the necessity) of further determination, but this further determinateness is not explicitly given as such, but exists only in the form of a promise; the contact thus gives a determinateness contextualized by a shroud of indeterminacy, an aura of invitation or what James J. Gibson calls "affordance." The subsequent development of the contacts will be the making—the becoming—of actual determinateness along the indeterminate paths projected by the initial determinacies. Advancing along these paths is the process of the coming into being— the coming into developed specificity—of both object and subject. In the

myriad everyday encounters we have with specific objects and environments, these explorations and developments advance our contact in
small, incremental ways, but in sufficient quantity, such developments
precipitate qualitative changes in the very character of our contact. This
advance, this learning in which the very identity of the subject-object
contact develops, is the process of habituation.

At root, how we perceive the significance of things is always in terms
of what Edmund Husserl calls an "I can," that is, the determinateness of
our experience is always a product of evaluation, and the terms of the
evaluation are the ways it is possible to have bodily interaction. Through
practicing our bodily behaviors, what we can do becomes more sophisticated. Through our actions we explore beyond our familiar zones of contact into what are initially the strange frontiers "beyond" our immediate
grasp, and repetition of such actions allows us to establish new dimensions of familiarity within these formerly strange arenas of experience.
With familiarity comes inconspicuousness, that is, various practices,
once they become familiar, come to operate for us without explicit reflection or self-conscious control. The development of habits is essentially the development of our bodily behavior to a state in which the
pattern of behavior has become sufficiently familiar to function automatically. When this practice can run automatically, two results follow.

The first result of habituation is that our directed, focused attention
is freed up to direct and focus attention onto new tasks. When we are
building habits, we must focus all our attention on executing specific, un-
familiar behaviors in which our body relates to a situation or object as to
an alien; successfully building the habit means having this activity incor-
porated into ourselves in such a way that it no longer requires paying attention to it. Once habituated, the body no longer encounters an alien
object with which it must contend, but rather inhabits that object and
lives out of that contact, in such a way that, as William Faulkner writes
in *The Unvanquished*, "within the wrists and elbows lay slumbering the
mastery of horses" (p. 173). The habit, then, provides us with a new basis
of comfortable behavior in the context of which we can work on performing new actions. The habit allows us to free our explicit attention
from the more primitive task, and to devote it to some different practice.

The second result of habituation is that, because we can now perform the first operation automatically, the environment within which we
pick for ourselves a second task to which to attend is more sophisticated
than the environment within which we picked the first task; developing

an habitual ability to walk erect, for example, makes possible for the first time engaging in the practice of running or playing hopscotch or performing a ballet routine. This pattern of development by which we open up for ourselves more sophisticated possibilities through developing a comfortable familiarity with more basic engagements is visible throughout human life, but it is especially visible with infants: watching a child grow is precisely watching an intelligent body—an interpreting, synthesizing body—come to master, step-by-step, the practices necessary to function as a fully formed human, and what is very noticeable is the way children move through sequences of first learning a more primitive ability and thereby making possible the development of a more complex ability. In each case, the child moves from acting in a way that aims at the desired behavior to actually being able to perform a rough version of the behavior, to becoming adept at the behavior through a repetition in the course of which the behavior becomes smoother and more perfect precisely as it becomes automatic and inconspicuous. Habituation, then, is the process by which we build up within our bodily life progressively more sophisticated degrees of inconspicuous behavior, such that the "I can" with which we make contact becomes progressively more complex with respect to the object contacted and the agent contacting.

Now if we think back on our earlier discussion of the terms in which to understand the substance of the body—trespass, pleasure, shame, and seduction—what we can notice in this account of habituation is that our very body is what is developing through the process of habituation. Our bodily existence is not something to be weighed and measured mathematically, but is that through which we contact the world, that which can be violated. As we develop habits, it is precisely the referent of these expressions ("that through which we contact," and "that which can be violated") that changes. An outside, scientific observer (i.e., an observer suffering from all the prejudices we have so far diagnosed and rejected) might well describe a certain situation as a human body being clothed and sitting at a desk with a computer; described as the living experience it is, however, the situation does not allow itself to be partitioned in this way. For the living bodily agency under observation, the shoes are as much a living part of itself as the feet, and the computer can be just as much a functioning organ of the bodily "I can" as the hands. Indeed, the house or office in which the typing is taking place can be absolutely central to the person's sense of comfort and safety, and can be a greater point of vulnerability for trespass and self-display than that person's shoulders or face as, for example, when one feels personally violated after a burglary. In other words, there is not an organic body with clothes and computer added; rather, the whole assemblage of organism-clothes-computer *is* the living body. When we give up our familiar prejudice of mind-body dualism, then, we must also give up our familiar prejudices about what are the phenomena that constitute the body.

The Subject-Object as "I can"

We saw at the end of chapter 1 that human reality is "the subject-object pair," the very situation that is the occurrence of meaningfulness. In this chapter we have understood this subject-object situation as the body, and we can now see that this means that the subject-object is the "I can." To be a body, a subject-object, is to be a being of possibility, a being open to the emergence of determinateness from an horizon of indeterminacy. The hand is a determinacy the very definition of which is to make grasping possible—it is that by which I can grasp—and as such it is a route that opens us to a multitude of as yet unimagined experiences. This is the situation of the body as a whole—it is the determinateness that opens us to an indeterminate multiplicity of possibilities, of which our action is the actualization. The development of the human is the development of this "I can." We are what we can do, and the identities of those things that we contact are measured in terms of these abilities. We are our possibilities for interactions with things, and things are their possibilities for our interaction.

In chapter 1, we studied the place of interpretation in the identities of the objects of our experience. We can now see more clearly that this interpretation is not some free-floating act of intellectual assessment, but is the response to an environment in terms of our determinate bodily capacities. It is how we are as bodies that sets the terms for our interpretation—our appropriation—of our environment. To be an object can only mean to be meaningful in terms of our bodily possibilities. Now this might seem odd when we consider objects like moral values (things we "should" do); intellectual principles (rules of logic or mathematics, or perhaps philosophical concepts); or aesthetic norms (beauty or "good taste"). Nonetheless (as we shall begin to see later), these objects are also defined in terms of bodily capacities, but the capacities of very developed and habituated bodies.

It is not hard to recognize that to call something "a chair" is a shorthand way of saying "I can sit there," or, given the more complex relations into which we tend to place chairs, "I can sit there while others are present without looking stupid," "I can put it in my kitchen in such a way that I can still move around," and so on. Most simply, a chair answers to our bodily posture and characteristic bodily behavior, and even in those more complex relationships that we in our society typically demand something measure up to in order to be called "a chair," the determinants of identity are still structures of our bodily "I can." Similarly, a pencil is simply that with which I, a body with hands, can mark some other substance, paper is that upon which I can leave my mark, and so on. The key to seeing that this is also the case in the more sophisticated moral and intellectual objects is already hinted at in what we have here seen about the chair. One requirement for something receiving the title "chair" can be that others will recognize it as such, or, as I just put it, I will not appear to them to be stupid if I deem it a chair. This last point reminds us that our dealings with things in the world are typically interwoven with our dealings with other people, and that an essential aspect of what my body can do is to encounter such others, and we will see, in fact, that it is this relation to others like ourselves that opens up the moral, aesthetic, and intellectual realms. This experience of other persons will need to be understood in light of the body's openness, which we have already considered, to what is "other" in general.

Our discussion of the body has emphasized the body as our original determinacy, our determinate capacities for interaction. Yet this very determinacy, these very possibilities, are possibilities for encountering other determinacies, other powers. To define the body as our point of contact and as our inherent publicity, is to recognize that to be a body is to be subjected to other determinacies. To be a body is to experience ourselves as subjects, that is, to find ourselves subject to the specificities and demands that usher both from the forms in which we are open and from the forms of that upon which we open. In this sense, then, the very nature of the body is to be defined by the point of view of others, that is, to be defined by how it is open to others, what it is for others. Because, therefore, the initial determinacy of the body is precisely a determinate openness, our basic determination is to be determined by others, or, we might say, the fundamental demand we place on others is that they place demands on us.

What this means is that the value of "the other"—that which is outside my immediate control and places demands upon me—is inherent to our embodiment: to be a human body is to make contact, which is to be such that what matters to the other already matters to me. The fundamental capacity of our body—the fundamental capacity that is our body—is the capacity to care about the others, where "others" runs the full range from inert things to other persons. This is the amazing fact of experience, of "being-there" ("*Dasein*"), as Martin Heidegger says: we are *aware* of, we are affected by, others, and *we retain our identity by being absorbed in the identities of our surroundings*. As we have seen, then, awareness, cognition, or knowledge is of the essence of embodiment, for knowledge just is this recognizing—this measuring up to—the determinacy—the demands—of what is other.

We will see later that the values of aesthetic, moral, and intellectual life are just the more sophisticated developments of this fundamental capacity, this fundamental "I can": "I can care about what others care about." To interpret is to see something *as* something, to bodily engage with something in terms of some accessible determinacy, and to see something not just idiosyncratically but in its universal significance—the issue behind truth—is to see it *as* it is open to another perspective that I, or another body like me, can adopt. The demands for objectivity and universality that are the core of our moral, artistic, and scientific values are just the demands to respond to things as they can matter to others and not just as they happen to matter to me according to my singular whims. The ideals of truth, beauty, and goodness are the ideals to which we can aspire because of our fundamental bodily capacity to care. These ideals are implicit in the very notion of care, and our artistic, moral, and intellectual life is just the explicit taking up of these values to which we can respond by virtue of being sensitive. By virtue of being the activity of making contact, the body is the activity of subjecting itself to an other to which it must answer, and the specific objects we encounter in our engagement with the "absolute" values of truth, beauty, and goodness are simply the revelation of way in which we as sophisticated, habituated bodies have come to develop our capacity to encounter the inherent richness of the determinateness "other."

This theme of universality, which derives from the inherently public character of our body as "making contact," thus raises the issue of intersubjectivity, of social and interpersonal life. These issues of intersubjectivity will soon be our explicit focus, for we will see that the issue of other people is not simply one issue among many, but is rather the issue that sets the terms for all our dealings. Before addressing the place of other people in our lives, however, we can study more directly the constitution of the identity of this habitually elaborated, interpretive

body-subject and especially the correlation of this with the establishment of the identity of a determinate world within which this subject is
situated. We can study, in other words, how the development of the
identity of the subject and the development of the identity of the object
are paired processes (and we will go on to see that this development of my
subjectivity-objectivity is inseparable from the development of my involvement with other people and their developing projects of subjectivity-
objectivity).

In our study so far, we have seen that it is our being habituated to developed modes of behavior that opens up to us the more complex forms
of objective life. We can turn, now, to the phenomena of memory to see
how the past—the habituation—is carried forward and made present in
the form of the object.

3
Memory

Location, Specificity, and Temporality

At any moment, I find myself located. I find myself located in a specific situation that has a thickness to its identity that runs off in many directions, reaching a kind of indeterminateness beyond those points to which I pay direct attention. As I sit typing, I can look out my window onto the yard, and beyond the yard to the neighboring houses, each of which contains a family, and has another yard behind it. I can anticipate the day when this book will be finished, as I can remember the last time I began writing a book. I feel the tiredness in my eyes and my feet that comes from not having slept enough in the last few weeks and not having started this writing early enough in the day, and I very much feel like putting aside the task of writing. I can notice the steady ticking of the clock somewhere behind me; I can hear the birds chirping outside. I feel heat in my face that I know comes from having just been drinking a cup of hot coffee, the taste—but mostly the acidity—of which vaguely lingers inside my mouth. Attending to that makes me think of kissing. While I type, the scenes of a recent romantic trip selectively replay themselves, woven together with scenes of another similar trip. I am located in relation to this romantic project, and I wonder vaguely, but excitedly, how this project will develop in the next short while. I am located in relation to the front yard, a yard that looks interesting, but with which it is in fact boring to do anything other than gaze at it. I am located in relation to my limbs and their weary heaviness (in the case of my legs) or their keen agility (in the case of my fingers). I am located in relation to my romantic partners and the activities we share, to my neighbors and their prejudices, to my readers, whom I do not know (and never will), and with all of these people I have a concern about how I will appear to them. At any moment, my experience is located in relation to all these directions of significance, all these contacts, these "senses." All of the determinations of my experience stretch out from me in these many dimensions—interpersonal, visual, organic, and environmental, all of which are of course spatial and temporal—and they populate my consciousness quite animatedly and emotionally. Whatever is meaningful to me is meaningful to me in terms of these and other similar modes of contact.

All of these significances that populate my consciousness are quite specific, which means that at any time there are only certain particular determinations with which I am explicitly engaged. This is precisely what it means to say that I am located, namely, that I am here and not there, that this and not that is what I am experiencing. To be an experiencer, to be a body—a bodily subject-object—is always to be determinate, specific, particular. This inherent specificity, this locatedness, is well-articulated in such novels as *Ulysses* by James Joyce or *The Sound and the Fury* by William Faulkner, which build their narrative from a description of the determinate flow of experience as it is lived by the experiencing subject. In these novels, the narrative is not told from the perspective of some all-seeing observer, but is articulated as the multiplicity of local, personally meaningful engagements that constitute the ongoing development of experience. Indeed, I can never be a "consciousness in general," as if I were an omniscient narrator of my own world, but I am always a specific assemblage of determinate engagements that are presently underway. And, while it is true, as we saw at the end of chapter 1, that I can be engaged with my world in terms of its universal significance (i.e., its significance for the other points of view that a person could adopt but that I am not in fact adopting), I can never vacate the particularity of my location. In other words, the very body that lets me be with others also demands that I always be this unique and specific one, this one from whom other possible stances are actually excluded.

My location—where I am now—is ontologically first, in that it is a point of reference in relation to which I must define myself; it is a first, however, that immediately defers to the firstness of another, namely, the past: my location is always premised on there having been another before. I always experience myself as having already been. It is as someone remembering that I am able to be here, and it is as something remembered that there is a here. What I remember, though, is always remembered as a promise, a route to a future; indeed, the memory that I have terminated my lease and that I will have to move in six weeks is inscribed for me in every determination of this apartment, which I have only just moved into. I feel as if I cannot settle. The very past to which the present defers its firstness, defers its own firstness in turn, announcing the future as the real point of definition for my location. Yet this future is my future, the future of the me who is present now. The future, too, defers its primacy, like the past and the present, for the future rests its existence on my actions now. This is the irreducible temporality of our existence, the equiprimordiality of the past, present, and future that is constitutive of our identity.

Just as the determinations of my situation afford different routes for development so is that the case in that particular mode of engagement that is the self-conscious imaginative exploration of my experience. The significances that orient my consciousness are quite specific but, like the body itself, they are specificities that point beyond themselves to further possibilities, further developments. I can, in other words, turn my attention to these determinations and explore them further. As we have seen through our consideration of temporal structure of interpretation and especially through our consideration of habit, the determinations that orient me are established significances that are handed over to me from my past. They are the locating memories, and they exist as performing a function of contextualizing, but they do not appear explicitly in their full force. Thus, even though they are me—they are the very substance of my consciousness and figure how I engage my environment—I have to investigate in order to find out who I am. They—my matrix—must come to be known by me through a time-consuming, explicit project of development along routes of inquiry that are initially given only as indeterminate invitations. We have already seen that the history of contact is what sets these parameters. All of these determinations are the figurings of our contact; all are determinations of our developed, complex "I can." They are bodily engagements that define determinate subject-object splittings—relations of a here where I am to a there where I am not—that point beyond their immediate determinatenesses to indeterminate horizons for further exploration (a family I can meet, a yard I can walk in, a book I can pick up off the shelf, etc.). Reflection on these determinations is itself one of the activities "I can" pursue. We see here that these parameters are always lurking, orienting us, and we have to work to find out what they are.

This further exploration of the contextualizing determinations that fill my consciousness is creative, and in some ways the attention I pay to these determinations resembles my writing a story. If I attend to any one of these determinations, for example, the taste of the coffee, I will begin to trace in thought a route leading to a consideration of sitting in the kitchen with my coffee mug and to a consideration of my roommate with whom I was talking at the table, and to the travel plans we spoke about, and so on. This further exploration amounts to constructing a narrative that is itself a selective actualization of the various possibilities for further thinking that are lurking in my experiential location. This exploration can be fanciful or it can be very compelling—I feel like I have to follow some idea through—and it can be very demanding (if, for example, I am trying to remember just what a friend said, and I have to work to get it right). My own experience is a determinate setting with horizons for possible exploration, and this determinateness sets the same demands as any other determinateness, namely, it must be addressed according to the (time-consuming) demands that it projects.

I am engaged with these specific determinations that characterize my location, and these determinations offer themselves as points of departure for further exploration, though what will be found through exploration is not immediately available to me as a determinateness already there in my awareness but exists, rather, as a promise, an aura of expectation that permeates each determination. Indeed, the promise of each expectation is somewhat like the way this very writing I am doing promises to become the beginning of a longer work, itself not yet written but already present in this experience of writing as "on the way." This investigation into what is lurking in my experience is itself a determinate—and present—task, that is, it takes time and commitment and has rules and problems. To do this will mean not to do other things. It is a creative and constructive pursuit that amounts to my decision about how to live my life with others now. It is a present task, it is a task built toward the construction of a narrative that will be realized in the future, and above all it is a task founded in my relationship to my past.

The present, future-oriented decision to explore the significances that lurk at the edges of my experience is a decision to practice a kind of history or archaeology. This lurking—the way in which the details of my experience are "forgotten," that is, not immediately present to me—is the fundamental phenomenon of memory, that is, it is as forgotten that we remember our past. Though this attempt to self-consciously determine what our location is (rather than simply being located) by calling, into explicitude what lurks within our experience is what we normally call "remembering" it might better be specified as "writing history" (in these examples practiced in a relatively arbitrary and idiosyncratic way, but admitting of many degrees of sophistication and systematicity). In other words, the explicit practice of self-conscious remembering rests upon a more fundamental sort of remembering that is precisely not self-conscious. Our ability explicitly to become conscious of—to "remember"—the past thus rests on a more fundamental way in which our bodies do not allow the past simply to be past, but maintain its presence as the unconsciously orienting structures of significance within experience.

I want to focus on this continuing presence of the past in human existence, and to consider the demands that this side of our temporality makes in our attempts to live out our lives. We have already seen that it is our habits that fundamentally shape and figure our subject-object contact. Our habits are the way we carry our past along with us: in habits we remember ourselves, but in the form of a forgetting. Such forgotten memories are what constitute our human identities, giving us the determinatenesses from which it is possible to project a future, and I want now to consider more explicitly this constitutive role of memory in human identity.

Memory and Objective Form

Where is memory? Memory is the very substance out of which the determinations of our world are built. We tend to think of memory as a picture gallery in our head, somehow embedded in brain cells; in fact, memory is the very "matter" of reality. While having brain cells may be a precondition for having memory, memory itself is to be found in the things that we experience, not in our heads. Memory is what locates us.

We tend to think of memory as an activity in which we explicitly conjure up for ourselves a thought of an earlier experience upon which we then reflect. There certainly is such a phenomenon of memory, but it is a secondary phenomenon. More fundamentally, our memory is at play in providing a constant background to our actions. I do not, for example, spend every moment of my day explicitly reflecting on my need to fill out some forms by the end of the day, but I certainly remember this. Throughout my day my actions all take account of their locatedness within a day in which those forms must be completed, even though the explicit thought of those forms passes before my mind only occasionally, and only when triggered by some specific circumstance. In chapter 1, we considered how it is that the acts of interpretive synthesis by which we have objects are not explicit acts performed subsequent to achieving a situation of encountering another, but are, rather, implicit in the very having of another. Memory, similarly, is an activity that is always at play in the very having of an experiential situation, and is not primarily an activity that occurs as a specific action within, and subsequent to, such a situation.

The memory that "I need to fill out forms," and the memory that "I need to move in August"—these are memories that present themselves in my experience as the inability simply to rest comfortably with my surroundings. These memories shape the very form of my experience, the very way I am sensitive to my surroundings—how things feel. As we have already seen, our identity is enacted as a directedness toward and absorption in, objects, and so it is primarily as a characteristic of objects that such memories are felt; our interpretive identity is, as it were, invested into the very form of things. More exactly, then, what presents itself in this situation is a room that does not allow me to be comfortable. I experience my surroundings as nagging me in some way, and this tension will only be released when I have actually concluded the task the memory of which haunts the situation. This can be developed more fully if we turn first to the notion of the past—what we remember—as "commitments."

In chapter 1, we developed the notion of the experiencing subject as one who has experience by virtue of remembering and expecting. To expect is to project a future; it is to be engaged with the present by being engaged toward something further. Our engagement with the present, then, is always done on behalf of, or in the service of, something further that does not yet exist except as or through our commitment to its realization. Our engagements, our contacts, then, always have as one of their constitutive dimensions a commitment to the realization of some goal. The past is the continuing presence of these commitments once the immediate engagements in which these commitments were made are no longer present. To carry out a project, one must remember that one is engaged in it, and the past is the continuing presence of how we have made ourselves beholden to the demands of specific projects. In this sense, then, the past exists for us as the way that we are not free in any situation simply to do whatever we like, but are always "already committed": we are already determinately underway with a number of projects of varying degrees of compellingness and our past is thus how we find ourselves bound.

Being bound here means that, because of the projects to which we have committed ourselves, there are limitations to what we can do while still retaining the identity we have made for ourselves. Our projects and our actions open us to a world, and this is a development of the "I can."

It is a development in the sense of making determinate, which means it is as much an introduction of limitation as it is an increase in power. The world we open up is opened up for us determinately or specifically, which means the form its identity takes carries within it the specificities of how our contacts are figured: the determinateness of the world becomes the bearer of our history, the inscription of the specificity to which we have committed ourselves. This determinateness of our contacts is the determinateness we experience as objects, and our memory of our projects—our very ability to retain our own identity—is carried by the objects upon which our body opens out. Our memory, most fundamentally, is what we experience *as* the determinateness of objects that communicates to us what we can and cannot do. Our objects, rather than our brain cells, are the "files" that retain our past. They offer themselves as things in relation to which we face commitments, demands. It is the things that are the determinateness of my situation that announce in their very identity—their very responsiveness to my bodily "I can"—the limitations and the demands that my past commitments place upon me. These objects are the carriers of my promises. Not only, then, is memory not primarily reflective and occasional but instead implicit and pervasive; it is, furthermore, primarily an objective phenomenon, that is, a determination of objects, not of subjects.

Remembering, then, is at the core of the experience of having objects. The general activity of maintaining a world is the general activity of implicit, pervasive remembering. What we perform when we engage in a self-conscious, reflective act of explicit remembering is not an introspective rummaging through past mental files, but is a present explication of the significance implicit in the identities of the objects with which we are engaged. This is why, for example, we can often remember something by returning to the location where we thought of it earlier: by interacting with the object themselves we will likely notice and make explicit the same sides of their identities as we did the first time. Marcel Proust, in *Swann's Way*, describes well this way that objects carry our memories when the narrator tastes for the first time a pastry dipped in tea that he had not eaten since his youth:

> And as soon as I had recognised the taste of the piece of madeleine soaked in her decoction of lime-blossom which my aunt used to give me . . . immediately the old grey house upon the street, where her room was, rose up. . . . [A]nd the whole village of Combray and its surroundings, taking shape and solidity, sprang into being, town and gardens alike, from my cup of tea. (51)

In his encounter with this particular object, the whole former self-and-world complex to which this object belonged is unexpectedly returned to the narrator, because the very identity of the object is a reflection of the subject-object contact of which it was a development.

Memory, whether implicit or explicit, is an act of present cognition in which we make explicit the identities of objects in terms of how they carry for us our commitments. Our ongoing behavior, in which we respond to the determinate identities of the objects of our world, is an ongoing reliance upon, and maintenance of, our implicit memory of our own selves, while our explicit, reflective remembering, is a self-conscious elaboration of this tacit self-recollection that is embedded in the significances of these objects. It is by building habits that we establish a determinate identity in the world, and establishing habits involves making the concerns that drive our involvements inconspicuous. Memory is effectively the recognition of what has been concealed through the process of habituation, either implicitly in our practical discriminations within our environment, or explicitly through self-conscious acts of reflective explication of this implicit significance of our situation. It is primarily *as objects* that our memory is enacted, and it is thus *as objects* that our identities are primarily embodied: who we are is how we establish the identity of our world, and remembering about ourselves means learning about objects and the identities we have built for them and for ourselves through our habitual embodiment. Having a coherent world is primarily how we implicitly remember who we are, and reflective memory is how we make explicit this identity through the explicit unfolding of the layers of habitual interpretation that constitute the identities of our objects.

As we have seen in chapters 1 and 2 with respect to experience, self-identity, and embodiment, so also with respect to memory a proper description of how we experience requires that we replace our typical ways of thinking with a conception that is radically different from, and in some ways diametrically opposed to, our familiar prejudices. It is by *being* the identity of objects that we exist, and explicitly to remember is to decipher in an act of present explication of the world that we face what of ourselves we have embedded into our objects. Our ability to continue to be ourselves is our ability to maintain a continuity and integrity to the objects of our world: our own identity is as coherent and enduring as is our world, the living presence of our past. Explicitly to remember is to open up what is latent in the significance of our objects, and in so doing to discover our own past as the commitments that have shaped our identities.

As conscious beings, we are characterized by "intentionality," that is, we are directed toward objects. We do not initially notice ourselves explicitly, but notice only our surroundings. Our study of memory reveals that this not-noticing of ourselves—this absorption in our world—is the fundamental form of our self-consciousness, that is, in having a coherent world, we implicitly know ourselves; we rememer who we are. In the study of moods we can take account further of this our "objective" self-consciousness.

Mood

We have talked about the distinction between our implicit, pervasive memory and our explicit, occasional memory. The latter is experienced as reflective thought. How is the former experienced? What is the form of experience of the immediacy of the embodiment of our commitments as objects, the form of our fundamental route to self-consciousness? This experience is what we call "mood." It is how we feel that offers our fundamental take on the basic reality of things, which means the basic commitments we have made in our project of contact.

It is another typical prejudice of ours that our moods are of secondary significance, and that, for example, we should learn to think without them. We sometimes mark out specific individuals as emotional and others as unemotional. We urge people to "be rational," and not to respond "emotionally." We typically treat our emotions as a separate sector of our experience, one that misleads us when it comes to apprehending the truth. Once again, our prejudices mislead us. Rather than being of secondary significance, our moods are our primary way of knowing reality; they provide the foundation for our more developed and reflective acts of knowing. Indeed, as Martin Heidegger says in *Being and Time*, "[T]he possibilities of disclosure belonging to cognition fall far short of the primordial disclosure of moods in which Dasein is brought before its being as the there," that is, it is our moods that initially open us into the world, and rational, reflective life is itself one of the developments of our moods, rather than a separate access to reality (p. 127).

Just as we cannot get away from our bodies, we cannot get away from our moods. To be related to a situation is always to be in some mood or other. It is easy to imagine being in the wrong mood to carry out a complex process of reasoning, and in imagining how we would have to feel instead, we can see very clearly that reasoning requires a very specific mood. The mood required for rational discourse is a mood of calm, but also a mood enthusiastic about pursuing the implications of various ideas and so on. It is not ultimately tenable to distinguish some people as emotional from some who are not, or some experiences as being emotional and some not. Our mood is the specific way we feel about our world; it is our immediate grasp of beings as a whole. Moods are our immediate sensitivity, the immediate way in which we experience the demands of objectivity. Moods are how we feel the presence of objects.

In a mood, how we are is certainly manifest, but it is not manifest *as* a self-perception. To be in a mood is to have objects appear in a certain way. When I am bored, I experience things in the world as dull and uninviting—as boring. It is the things that fail to engage me and offer me exciting routes of action. When I am angry, things are invasive and challenging to my rights and to my personal space. When I am excited, things seem electric, and charged with possibility. When I feel amorous, the world seems enchanted, precious, and welcoming. In each case, to experience the mood—to be "in" the mood—is to have objects in a certain way. The mood is how the world gathers itself up and shows itself to me.

To experience the world as having a certain flavor (and I think it is noteworthy that vocabularies of taste and touch tend to be among our richest resources when we want to describe how things feel to us in different moods), is to have certain paths of action more or less ready. Moods open certain paths and close others, or, better, they clear certain paths and obscure others. In anger, it is hard to see how the world can be trusted, or how it can be something with which one can cooperate, or even that one can tolerate. In sadness, it is hard to see how various tasks can be worth doing. In love, it is hard to see how this other person could ever be someone of whom to be critical. In tranquillity, it is hard to see how the world could ever warrant an unbalanced response. Moods are the way in which whole paths of action are closer or farther from us, not in a geometrically measurable sense, but in a "felt" sense, that is, in the sense of being real possibilities for our existence. In moods it is not impossible to go down the obscure routes, just as it is not impossible to be a musician with only three fingers, to make a fist in a pink room, or to keep writing even when one needs to sleep, but the general tone of things directs us elsewhere. It is not impossible to take the obscure routes, but everything in the world speaks against it, and it requires work, and perhaps practice, to be able to follow these paths. Indeed, actually following these difficult paths may result in a change of mood, when opening the unexpected dimensions of the situation results in the situation feeling different. Moods open up the situation as a whole—give a flavor to the world—and offer paths for uncovering—advancing into—the more precise determinations and articulations that are the things within this world.

In saying that moods are a determinate stance toward objectivity, it is implied that moods are inherently articulate and intelligible. The mood is an interpretive stance that we take toward our situation as a whole, and like any interpretive stance it involves projecting expectations about what will happen, and being oriented toward a direction of action for oneself. In being in a mood one is making a claim, that is, the way objects feel is an expression of the stance of one's being-in-the-world. Because they are experienced as the form of objects, however, we do not recognize in moods the expression of ourselves, that is, we do not see our moods as our most primitive self-reflection, here carried out in the very identities—the very style of existing—of our objects.

Even though our moods are complex and subtle and have an inherently intelligent structure, they present themselves to us as immediate "intuitions"—as, literally, a direct "feel" for the situation as a whole. To make explicit their articulateness requires work because they present themselves to us as the seamless immediacy that is the very tissue of reality. The typical inarticulateness of our expressions of mood—"I feel bad," or "I feel sad"—captures this immediacy, that is, it captures the way in which the mediation—the intelligibility—of the mood is not experienced discursively, but is experienced all at once as a whole, and as a whole that is "the way things just are," and not a way in which "I" am "doing" something, not a way in which I could intervene and find my own projective, synthetic structures at the core. We call a mood an "emotion" or a "pathos" to indicate the sense in which we experience ourselves as moved by the world, as passive in the having of the mood. In moods, we experience ourselves as undergoing the self-showing of the way of the world, and our experience is one of submitting to—of being affected by—our objects, not as acting. In moods, the general tone of things feels forced upon us.

As interpretive stances upon our situations of contact, however, moods need to be understood in basically the same ways as our more reflective stances of interpretation. We could call moods the "immediacy of interpretation." Mood and interpretation are not separate spheres of our existence; rather, we exist interpretively, and mood is the fundamental way in which interpretive existence is experienced by us. Every way we interpret is a way of feeling things, and every way of feeling things is a way of interpreting. What we have seen about interpretation is that it lets the present be present by virtue of being projective and recollective, and so we must see in our moods a presenting that is the immediacy of this dynamism of projection and recollection. In our emotional life we must recognize the immediate tissue of our experience of the world in terms of our projects and our memories. The projection and recollection that has become for us an immediate structure of experience is a habit.

We said that memory is the re-cognition of what has been concealed through a process of habituation. It is by building habits that we accustom ourselves to sophisticated modes of contacting, and the key to something becoming habitual is that it makes a more sophisticated action possible by making its own more primitive behavior automatic and inconspicuous. Habits, in other words, are structures of repression, structures in which we refuse to acknowledge what we are actually doing and, indeed, develop this refusal to the point that recognition of what we are doing is not in our power. Though it is a repression, that is, an occlusion of vision, the structure of habit is still very much a structure of memory; indeed, it is the most fundamental remembering, a remembering that is precisely a forgetting. We can have reflective memory by engaging in a present act of explicating the significance that is latent in the objects of our experience, but our implicit and pervasive remembering is the experiencing as a familiar immediacy the habitual figures we have developed for interpreting—interacting with—our situation. We become habituated to structures of recollection and anticipation, which is to say that we commit ourselves to certain narratives about what we will recognize as the determinacy of our situation and what we project on its horizon. It is *as* the determinacy of our situation that this repressed structure of anticipation and recollection is remembered. If, to take a simplistic example, one has become habituated to coping with one's interpersonal life through fighting (if, say, that is the only way one's parents would allow one to have what one desires) then it is in terms of the demands of a fighting life that one will view situations. If one has become habituated to fighting over how one must eat one's dinner, then one may find that one often feels despondent around dinner time, or when faced with plates and cutlery. This immediate feeling would be an implicit remembering that "I will now be refused" or something similar. Or, again, an innocent question from a friend during a meal may be experienced as a threatening feeling of transgression against which one must protect oneself. In such ways, our developed moods are the immediate presentation of how we believe we should "expect" based on habitual commitments.

What we have now seen is that the objects of our world are sketched for us by our bodily "I can." The developing of a coherent identity as a whole is paired with the developing of a sense of a world as a whole, and the articulation of that world in so many specific objects is equally the articulation of our own self. The world and its constituent objects are fundamentally structures of the memory of the forms of this "I can" and its habituation and development into a familiar "being-at-home" as a stable person in a stable setting. Thus, in our present engagement with the world of objects we are fundamentally continuing to engage with our own past. Fundamentally, it is as mood, as an immediate, inarticulate intuition, that we experience the basic forms of how we have become stable selves-in-a-world.

We can turn now to consider the most important kinds of habitual contacts that we establish in giving substance to our lives: habits of interpreting and interacting with other people. Throughout we have been considering the importance of structures of familiarization in the development of human identity and we must now look at the dynamics of intersubjective familiarity. It is from this point that we will be able to understand the dynamism at the core of human development and to understand how we can speak of issues of health and disease, truth and error, in the context of human development. We will then be prepared to study the phenomena of so-called "mental illness."

Part II

The Substance of Human Experience

4

Others

Other People

In part I, we considered ourselves as projective (future), embodied (present), and remembering (past). This remained a formal study, though: we know that these structures are true of all human experience, but we have not yet recognized the core of human experience—what it is that marks it as human. We know that we are always involved in projects, but we do not yet know which projects. Are these interpretive projects simply arbitrary, as ancient skepticism says, or is there a universal human nature, as Aristotelian naturalism says? The skeptical position suggests that we have a fundamental freedom, the ability to define for ourselves who we are. The Aristotelian position insists on the determined character of our existence, the fact that being something human is something specific. We will see that in a sense each is right: fundamentally we are free, self-defining agents, but this very freedom has a determinate character of its own. Freedom, that is, by its very nature as freedom, sets up for itself demands to which it must attend and criteria by which it must act. Immanuel Kant argued that there are certain universal and necessary features that must be met by any experience *in order to be experience*, and we will see that something like this is so, though in a somewhat different form from the one for which Kant argued. We will see that human interpreters—free, self-determining, bodily agents—are fundamentally involved in an intersubjective project of mutual recognition or confirmation, and that it is this that provides the core to the formation of our identities, whether healthy or neurotic. The real substance of our lives is to be found in our dealings with other people.

We saw in chapter 3 that it is primarily the objects with which we are engaged that carry within their identities the commitments that form our identities. We will now see why, in particular, it is the objects we identify as other people that put upon us the primary demands that shape our distinctive human personalities. Within the world of our experience, we differentiate different kinds of objects: we differentiate plants from animals, from furniture, from art, and so on. As we have seen, these different types of object are so many different *ways of experiencing*, that is, each is a particular brand of phenomenon, of making contact. What we will now consider is what it is that specifically marks for us the phenomenon "other person." What form is our contact taking such that we identify ourselves as in relationship to another person? We will see that the distinctive character of such an experience is that the object with which we are dealing makes a claim, equivalent to our own, to being the most important thing around; like ourselves, the other person is a center of value, and recognizes herself as such. Let us consider more precisely the form in which other things occur within our world, and the specific place of other people within this world.

As we just saw, to experience an object as an object is to experience it as something that makes demands upon one. An object presents itself as a unity, as a thing that has an intrinsic integrity that accounts for the coherence of the multiplicity of specific features that characterize it, the variety it gathers into a singularity. In its own way, a thing announces itself as a center of meaningfulness that must be respected by whomever approaches it. At the same time, however, most things stand toward us as subordinate to our powers. We can move the chairs around, and they do not object; we can uproot the plant and it cannot overrule us. Even powerful beasts are subject to our control: through our technology and our cunning we can overpower them in direct conflict, and by learning of the demands of their life cycles we can prey upon their natural dependencies and compel them to subordinate their actions to our wills (a situation well-described in the second chorus of Sophocles' tragedy *Antigone*). There certainly are various ways in which all of these things can offer resistance, but at a fundamental level we experience ourselves as able to overpower them. Indeed, this openness of the thing to our ability to overpower it, to reshape it, is the core of that experience of "I can" that marks the object of our experience as "a thing," an identity already vulnerable to our ingress, to our identity.

We often try also to overpower other people. We order them around. We yell at them. We try to manipulate them by playing on their sympathy or fear. We humiliate them. It is interesting that we typically do not take up these latter strategies in our efforts to overpower nonhuman things. (Sometimes we do take up these practices, in relation to pets, for example, though in those cases we seem to model our behavior toward these things on our behavior toward humans. Such a confusion of practices properly directed at persons with practices properly directed at nonpersons is the core of Sophocles' tragic story of the madness of Ajax, the ancient Greek hero. Ajax, in his frustration at not being adequately recognized by his companions, tries to win the recognition he believes himself to deserve through torturing animals that he confuses with his fellows. Subsequently unable to bear the realization of his confusion—his "madness"—Ajax commits suicide.) What is it that makes these particular strategies possible or even fitting when it comes to dealing with other people? Why do we try to humiliate others? Why do we not just uproot them or move them as we do plants and chairs?

This difference between the way we deal with human and with nonhuman others is explained by the fact that we recognize the other person—the one we are trying to overpower—as having a say in the matter, that is, we experience the other person as an object that has the capacity to control how we have ingress into its identity. What we experience that lets us describe an object as another person is not specifically that person's feature of having mass; it is not specifically that person's property of needing to eat in order to live. Both of these features do obtain in humans, but neither of these captures the distinctive feature that is the source of the integrity of the human identity. What is distinctive of the human identity, as we have seen in this book, is the structure of projective embodiment, that is, the other is a center of interpretive activity such that that other's subjectivity is constitutive of the significance of the things it encounters. What that means is that what is happening to the other cannot simply be measured from the outside. It is not simply up to us who are outside to say what is happening "inside" (which does not mean "within the other's head" but "within the identity of the objects that populate the other's world"), for our own action is for that other an object the meaning of which is shaped by that other's ways of making contact. We cannot simply overpower the other in the way we can overpower a plant, because "overpowering" is itself a significance—an interpretation—that can only be bestowed upon our action by the other person: if the other does not acknowledge being overpowered, then in an important sense the other is not overpowered. We recognize this, for example, when we encounter familiar stories of victims of torture who will not "give in," who will not allow the force applied to themselves to "count" as sufficient to let themselves be overpowered and subject to the controlling will of the torturer and her or his demands. The experience of "I can" that we label *other person* is thus in part this fundamentally limiting experience of an "I cannot." Like all objects, the object "other person" is an experience of a particular kind of demand. This demand, though, has the especially charged quality of being the demand to answer to that other's "I can." I may approach the other with the attempt to control, but the other may not experience this to be as compelling a demand as I intend it to be. Other people, then, are those others in whom I can have a shaping influence only by communication and cooperation, only by integrating my will—my freedom, my being as a projective activity of interpreting—with that other's will. Of course, such talk of "cooperation" does not mean that our dealings are always friendly or free from violence; on the contrary, violence and conflict are, as we shall see, pervasive within human experience. Nonetheless, our violent approach toward another can never determine its own significance from within itself alone. How my action impacts the other is fundamentally informed by that other's interpretive contact with my action. In the other person, my lived body—my making contact—engages with another body like its own, and my own ability to make contact—my "I can"—is partially but essentially shaped by the hands of the other, that is, it is from the other's power of contacting that my own embodiment receives its powers of contacting, of touching. Other people are those whom we cannot touch without their help.

To encounter another, then, is to encounter our own deficiency, our own incapacity. The other person is the necessary route along which I must pass in order to have access to the very world I open onto—my very own world. To be a person is to experience oneself as "the one to whom things matter," which means to experience oneself as someone who matters oneself, that is, I matter because I am that through which other things can matter. Yet to experience another is to experience one's own incapacity fully to live up to this sense one has of oneself, for, on my own, I do not sufficiently determine how things matter inasmuch as others, like myself, have equal—and competing—rights to assuming the same role, and especially to assuming that role with respect to this very question of the significance of myself and their selves. To be a person, then, is to be in the midst of other people, which means to be engaged in the project of needing to cooperate in order to determine what is the significance of *persons as such*. To be a person, in other words, is to be animated by the question, "What is a person?" that is, the question, "Who are we?"

As a single person, I experience others—I touch and am touched by others—as the demand to correlate my own sense that I matter with the potential challenge to that view that is the recognition that those others matter. It is my very sense of myself as someone who matters that is at issue in recognizing another as "another person," and thus to be a person is to be involved in a struggle to establish a secure sense of oneself, a sense that can be mutually recognized by both me and that other. This is an issue we never get over in our lives: it is the defining question that drives all our human experience. I and the other person both have at stake for ourselves the need to estimate our mutual worth: we must each coordinate our self-esteem with our estimation of the worth of the other (and with, therefore, our estimation of the other's estimation of ourselves and the other's self-estimation, and the other's estimation of these estimations, etc.).

One's body, then—the human body—is that fundamental authority for defining significance whose very project, when successfully pursued, leads to the recognition that this authority is subordinated to a greater authority, namely, the authority of the intersubjective domain the significance of which is not established without reference to the parallel fundamental authority of the other as the determining source of value. Thus, in a yet more powerful way than we have seen before, the body is a self-transcending reality (and we will go on to see this aspect further developed and specified with the family, and civil life). We initially defined the body as an openness to significance, and this receptivity of recognizing other persons is the strongest sense of this openness; it is, namely, an openness to the redefinition of this very openness precisely through the process of intersubjective contact.

To experience other people is to experience those whom we recognize to be capable of passing judgment upon us. It is equally true that we are beings who can pass judgment upon them, and it is furthermore true that this is how we are for them as well. What we have, then, is a variety of points of view, each of which has a legitimate claim to being able to say what the real significance is of our actions and the actions of others; our intersubjective world is constituted for us by this tension of having multiple points of authority, and the various forms our intersubjective life takes are the various determinate ways in which we try to resolve these problems of securing a sense, precisely, of who we are, of what we are worth, of how we matter—of establishing where the authority lies for determining the significance of our own efforts at determining significance.

Now, as we just said, we still do try to overpower others. Indeed, attempts at overpowering are our most immediate routes to trying to solve the problems these tensions of authority pose. Let us consider how this is so, and what the consequences of these strategies are. In particular, let us consider more clearly how the experience of another person is an experience of our inability to *force* that other to recognize the authority of our own perspective.

We are inherently open to other people. My actions need to be taken up by the other, but it is equally true that the other cannot fail to take them up, just as I cannot fail to respond to the other. We are never isolated individuals who only subsequently enter into contact with others. On the contrary, we are from the start inescapably engaged with the experience of other people. This is evident, for example, in the phenomenon of newly born children imitating the gestures of the people around them. The children do not go through a process of study, practice, and learning, but rather inhabit immediately the gestural comportment of the body that the adult is enacting such that the child lives its own body out of a kind of inherent sympathy for the adult's mode of behavior. This native sympathy for others, however, does not mean that our dealings with others are inherently smooth or happy; it means only that we inherently inhabit the interhuman sphere of communication and contact. In fact, this inherent sympathy for others is initially an openness to experiencing a kind of challenge.

The other person initially exists for us as a challenge to our ability to be the authority. Certainly, all of the objects of the world can present themselves in this way to the child, but it is the parents who first show themselves, among all such objects, to be the centers of authority that must be acknowledged. (Of course, some children do not live with parents. The point made here will still apply to them mutatis mutandis, and the way these changes can be significant will be implied by our studies in chapter 5.) Likewise, children appear to their parents as unlike dishes and furniture in that children have a will and an intellect, and they cannot easily be fit into neat plans: children are demanding. Typically, the relationship between children and parents is very much-a collision of wills. The parents and the children both have desires, and it is a sad truth that the resolution typically comes through a struggle to decide who has the stronger will. Parents may hit or restrain or otherwise assault their children. In doing so, they do not in fact defeat the will of the child, just as the victim of torture is not *directly* touched by the torturer's efforts to force compliance. Indeed, these measures do not even address the will, for they do not address the will *as will*, that is, they do not acknowledge that they are negotiating with an authority. Rather, these measures effectively "change the subject," announcing that "if you want to do that I will grip you tightly": these measures claim to be categorical imperatives—"you must . . ."—when in fact they are merely hypothetical structures—"if, . . . then. . . ." This change of subject is a show of force in which the parents show that they can divert the main feature of the situation to one in which their strength exceeds that of the child, and they effectively present the child with a *choice*, a situation in which the child must weigh the competing worths of various courses of action, even though the rhetoric of such gestures is to announce that the child has no choice.

Often, such a show of force is in fact successful in changing the focus of attention and in enticing the child to change the direction of her actions. But notice that there is no insertion of the parent's controlling power directly into the sphere of the child's will: it is the child's pragmatic assessment of the merits of the various possibilities within the situation that has determined the significance of the parent's actions. And the child, of course, may find that exactly the same strategy works for securing the desired result from the parents: the child may find that incessant yelling or peeing is unbearable to the parent. This, we should note, is not because yelling or urinating is unbearable in itself, but because that is the significance it has for the kind of contact that constitutes the identity of the parent; far from finding yelling and urinating unbearable, the child, in fact, probably relishes both activities, but can get its way because the parent estimates the worth of these actions differently than does the child. Here the child, like the parent above, has found a way to divert the central topic of their interaction from the manifest interaction concerning the unqualified ability to enact a recognition of the unique locus of authority to a tacitly cooperative negotiation concerning how to deal with a hypothetical imperative (an ultimatum), now conducted within a sphere in which the child has greater strength. Once again, there has been no direct taking over of the parent's will: there has just been a change of topic that was successful in soliciting from the parent the desired response.

With this parent and child, then, we have a conflict of desires that is resolved by various methods of successfully negotiating with the other by changing the topic of attention to one in which the one participant

acknowledges the superior strength of the other participant and this acknowledgment amounts to a willingness to let the other dictate the
course of subsequent behavior. Because it is the other person's willingness either to resist or to comply with the ultimatum that decides the
outcome of the situation, this situation cannot properly be described as
one in which one party is overpowered by the other. One may concede
defeat, and recognize oneself to be strategically outmaneuvered, but one
is not, strictly speaking, overpowered.

(It is, of course, essential to remember that this strategizing, calculat-
ing, conceding, and recognizing need not be—and typically is not—
explicitly recognized as such by the participants. This is the point of my
expression, "pragmatic assessment." The situation is an interpersonal negotiation, but a negotiation conducted behaviorally, pragmatically, and
not self-consciously. Indeed, even though what actually transpired was a
negotiation about hypotheticals, the manifest claim that this was an enforcement of power about categoricals may very well be the interpretation each party (wrongly) takes away from the engagement. Indeed, the
child (and, likewise, the parent) may very well take away from the negotiation a sense of her own weakness, and an interpretation of herself as
having been forced. Though her own will was essentially involved in the
situation, the child may not *recognize* that she "had a choice." Precisely
because of the child's lack of an education sufficient to allow it these developed self-recognitions, it remains important to recognize unjust ma-
nipulations of the power structures of such situations by parents, even if
it is not strictly true to say that the parents "force" the child's actions.)

I have chosen the example of the parent and child (and I will return
to it later) to note that this issue of dealing with other people confronts
us from the inception of our experience. The parent-child relationship is
certainly not the only kind of relationship in which we see these dynamics, however. In any and every sector of life, it is very often the case that
one person will engage with a second by using threats in some particular
sector of a relationship in which the second person deems herself to be
weak (i.e., the first person will set up an ultimatum, a hypothetical imperative) in order to win from the second person the specific recognition
that the first person is the authoritative power *simpliciter*. This is the prize
in such interpersonal struggles: what people want to win from one
another is the acknowledgment that they are the ones whose decision-
making, whose subjectivity, counts as the most important. This is not
surprising, since, as we have seen, it is this subjectivity that is definitive

of our identity as humans, and so what we want is simply to be recognized for what we are, or more exactly, for what we seem to ourselves to be. A husband will often insist that his wife recognize him as the dominant partner in the relationship. The wife will be required always to defer to his "better judgment" and to make her life over into one of service and support for his supposedly more important endeavors. A child who often loses out in similar struggles with his parents may well turn to a younger sibling or a playmate and apply pressure to the other child to engage in servile and submissive acts, in an attempt to counteract the challenge to her own centrality and autonomy that is encountered in dealing with the parents (and perhaps also to "beat" the parents by living a secret life outside their purview or an aggressive life that demonstrates their inability to control her.) These are common situations, and what is at issue in them are the roles of submission and domination. What is sought in these negotiations is recognition from the other that one is really the important one. The way in which we take ourselves to be the center of things has a path of development as well, and it is precisely the experiences we undergo through these struggles over authority that impel us down the path of collectively educating ourselves about the truth of who we are, as we shall go on to see.

Our humanity involves having a sense of ourselves, and what this sense of ourselves amounts to is a recognition that "I matter in the world." This sense needs to be confirmed by others, though, and in situations such as we have just considered, we try to win this confirmation by getting the other to confess that "You matter more than I do." As we have already indicated, though, such strategies have an inherent problem.

The goal in interpersonal struggles is to have one's importance recognized by the other. The strategies I have been considering, though, are ones in which this recognition is a comparative one in which the other must evaluate the competing claims to importance that come from herself and from oneself, and judge her own importance to be subordinate to one's own. There is a latent contradiction in such strategies, however, for in the very fact of needing and relying on this other's confirmation of my claim, my behavior has tacitly acknowledged that my sense of self-worth is contingent on that other's act of valuing; in other words, I reveal that the real thing that matters in the world is what is important to the other, not what is important to me. There is thus an incoherence to this way of taking up the project of contacting others, and it therefore cannot be the adequate way to resolve the problems of the experience of intersubjectivity.

What is really wrong with these strategies of domination is that they do not recognize the primacy of intersubjectivity—the primacy of the situation of mutual estimation that we have seen to be inherent to the human condition—but try instead to establish the primacy of the single isolated subject, as if that subject were sufficient on its own to establish the significance of its own reality. These kinds of dominating behavior, in other words, are built on interpretive strategies that cannot do justice to the objective demands of our engagements, and they will reveal their inadequacies at various points (as we shall go on to see). What they point to is the necessity for a situation of intersubjectivity that recognizes itself for what it is. A successful resolution to the tensions of intersubjective life requires that the single agents involved each come to recognize their own singularity and agency to be themselves premised on their participation in a larger human enterprise; it is in the project of cooperation, or, as well shall see, the project of mutual education, that the coherent form of intersubjective behavior is established.

This cooperation can be seen in a number of ways (the most constructive and powerful of which will be the subject of study in chapter 6), but, primarily, we see such cooperation in the situation we recognize as "a community," that is, collections of people adopting similar views about the order of things and consequently behaving toward each other out of a shared sense of what constitutes the reality of their world. In living according to shared codes, each member of a group tacitly announces in its behavior that what it takes to be authoritative is what the others who share the codes likewise take to be authoritative. In other words, by agreeing on a third thing—in this case, the principles upon which our world appears to us to be organized, the codes that we accept as authoritative for governing our practices—we agree with each other: in insisting on the authoritative character of the values that matter to oneself, one simultaneously acknowledges the authoritative character of what matters to the others. We will therefore see situations of cooperation and mutual recognition of identity in people who have (behaviorally) agreed upon a collective identity. In such a situation, the members have agreed upon the parameters for recognizing specific, personal identities by accepting to share an authoritative collective identity. To understand human subjectivity, then, we will have to study the ways in which people form a "we," that is, we have now to turn to human communities and to consider how they are the natural development of the interpretive project of making contact that defines our "I can."

Family

We saw that the elaboration of a contact involves developing a sense of who one is as a subject, just as much as it involves developing a sense of what the object is. It is our discoveries about what we can and cannot do in our contact with other people (and the overarching significance that this has for the significance of our "I can" in other contexts) that is the primary inducement to developing our sense of ourselves. If we initially start off with a sense of ourselves as the only important thing, we are quickly confronted with situations that deny this. The child must contend with the demands of objectivity, both in relation to those things that put up a relatively manageable resistance, and are mostly experienced as masterable and available, and in relation to those things—other people—that are actively and self-consciously resistant, and that put demands upon us in the very fundamental fashion of challenging our sense of our own status as sources of meaning and value. One has a continuing, bodily experience of the fundamental incapacity that defines us in our contact with other people when one finds oneself losing one's voice in front of an audience, when one feels the weight of another's judging eyes in the embarrassment that floods through the body, making one's skin burn, when one feels one's stomach aflutter in love or one's whole body energized in sexual passion, or when one's face is overtaken by an irrepressible smile in the sudden encountering of a cherished friend. In these situations, we feel in a very immediate way that we live in the midst of an intersubjective contact. Our own experiences give the lie to the sense of ourselves as the self-contained source of meaning. Our first sense of ourselves must be replaced by a more complex understanding of the self as involved in relations with other selves. (As we shall see, the central issue for development—for raising children—will thus be whether the child has a route constructed for her by her parents that allows her to develop appropriate options for self-interpretation; this growth needs to be "fed" as much as does physiological growth.) The cooperation identified above is thus a reflection or a consequence of the development of this new sense of self, or we could better say that this new mutually developed sense of self is a form of (intersubjective) contact that is embodied as particular forms of cooperative behavior.

The structure of cooperative self-definition that is most familiar is named for being such: the "family." When one understands oneself as a family member, one does not treat human importance as resting in one's isolated singularity—one's existence as this singular self—but as resting in one's particularity—one's existence as this particular role player among others in a shared situation. One does not regard oneself as the one and only significance, but as one significance among many: as a family member, one is one species—one example—of the important kind of person; for the family member, the truth is not "me," but "our thing" (*la cosa nostra*).

To understand the phenomenological significance of the family—to understand just what it means to people to experience themselves as family members, what kind of contact a "family member" is—it is probably helpful to think of families in a broader historical context than simply their appearance at the end of the twentieth century in the United States, for example. In contemporary America, the family is not the ultimate form in which intersubjective life is experienced, for the family experience is contextualized by its subordination to a larger, transfamilial culture. The human phenomenon of the family, however, does have its own proper cultural environment, that is, there can be a social environment that is defined by the primacy of the family. The family on its own terms functions and shows itself (in all its strengths and all its problems) only in certain situations. The phenomenon of the extended family as it shows itself in much of South American, Mediterranean, or perhaps Japanese culture probably comes closer to revealing the natural shape of the family than does the nuclear family of 1950s American television, and the structures of tribal and familial political struggle from ancient Greece, traditional Africa, or from pre-Columbian America display better still the logical form of the development of family life. (Indeed, we might see in the old mafia or the old yakuza forms of social life that would be better understood as the struggle of the institution of the family competing with the institution of modern political life than as "organized crime.")

I mention these various different types of family life because in the extended family or the tribe one sees much more clearly the sense in which people identify themselves with the identity of the family. For people who participate in these social environments, who one is, is primarily "being a member of the family." The logic of the family is, again, to take it as simply a fact that its identity is significant, and, indeed, the foundation of significance inasmuch as simply being a member of the family makes a particular person significant. Recognizing the family as family means recognizing it as the bestower of meaning, that is, recognizing it as the real agency that determines the ultimate "can" and "cannot," the ultimate interpreter of the significance of one's own interpretations of significance. This identity that one receives from the family, furthermore, is held in opposition to other identities, that is, participation in "our thing" is at odds with participation in activities in which one develops allegiances to other spheres that lay claim to reality such as other families or other social bonds. If the very basis of the family is that it appears to its members to be the bestower of signficance, then any other family can only be a rival, can only be a challenge to this central and defining orientation of the family. This is the basis of the phenomenon of the vendetta, that is, the vendetta is a natural structure of that form of making contact that is the family; in the vendetta structure we have something analogous to that struggle of one person with another that we identified in our examples of parent and child and of torturer and tortured. When the family is taken as the ultimate form of human cooperation, it can only experience other families as challenges, and it will be the natural life of each family to endeavor to realize its sense of its own primacy by establishing domination over other families.

Shakespeare's *Romeo and Juliet* offers a classic portrayal of the tensions between intrafamilial and extrafamilial loyalties, as lovers from two feuding families are destroyed because of the overarching demands of the family identity. It is because Romeo is a Montague and because Juliet is a Capulet that their attachment to each other will not be recognized as legitimate by either family. The family is here made the ultimate identity for interpreting the significance of social relationships, for determining the parameters of the "I can."

Ancient Greece offers a helpful case study of the pattern of development of such family life. Athens, for example, was governed by a small number of long-established extended families each of which sought to win preeminence in power over the others. It was here that our modern sense of a specifically "political" life emerged, in the struggles by which Athens sought to establish a system of social organization that denied to the family the right to identify itself as the primary social reality and to insist instead that the city—a social field built out of a variety of families—had to be recognized as worthy of the primary allegiance of all of its citizens, and that the city rather than the family would set the terms for legitimate and illegitimate action. Aeschylus' *Oresteia* illustrates well some aspects of this structure of family life, and especially the inherent problems that attach to this approach to establishing human identity. In this ancient Greek tragedy, Orestes, the son, must abandon his extra-familial life and return to deal with the demands of his family-based identity. His family values, however, lead him in opposed directions, for in order to carry out his familial responsibility to his father he must violate his familial responsibility to his mother. Specifically, he must avenge his father's murder—normally the familiar logic of a vendetta—but, since it was his own mother who killed his father, the vendetta-logic that aims to defend the family turns against itself in that Orestes must kill his mother and thereby destroy his family. The logic of the family, in other words, produces a situation in which it cannot preserve itself, and the terms it sets out for dealing with the demands of family identity are insufficient on their own to offer Orestes a noncontradictory course of action. The need to resolve this points to the need for something beyond the family and its vendetta-logic to govern human affairs, and the *Oresteia* ends with the emergence of a transfamilial council—the core of the idea of a "state"—that recognizes a larger sphere of social relations where family ties are not the ultimate ground for determining just action. An impartial lawcourt is established that is indifferent to issues of family membership in its evaluation of the significance of actions. While it must draw its participants from families, it is not as representatives of their families that the participants must judge; rather, they must recognize their own legitimacy as judges to be bestowed upon them by their acting on behalf of this impartial transfamilial society. In modern American society, this recognition of the family as subordinated to the "higher court" of larger political life has largely been accomplished, and the family as it appears in this society—the "nuclear" family—is the family that has taken on a form appropriate to its subordinate role.

The family, then, has a natural logic of its own, and this logic is not as immediately apparent in contemporary society as it is in societies where the family is taken to have greater claim to being the primary form of cooperative human endeavor. Rather than pursue further this aspect of the anthropology of the family, though, I want simply to take this understanding of the form in which the life of the family as a social institution naturally appears to our study of the phenomenology of the emergence of the sense of one's identity as a family member. These few historical and anthropological remarks will help us to know what to look for, and we will see in the phenomenology of family membership the ground for these very social structures and practices.

As we saw, establishing a secure sense of self comes with establishing a shared intersubjective sense of the nature of reality. It is thus through the support of other people that we are able to become familiar with the world. It is those who become our familiar others, the others through whom we become familiar with our world, who constitute our family. Just as our natural bodily organs—our hands, our mouth, and our legs— are the initial openings onto determinateness by which we grasp what it is "to be," by which we develop a sense for reality and what is possible in it, so do the determinate others into whose company we are born originate for us a route into that contact that is the "we." One's natural body is not an unbiased, universally uniform, fully transparent, or fully comprehensive accessing of reality, but is a perspectival, particular, opaque, and determinate hold on, posture in, and taste of being. We do not begin, as it were, fully connected to reality, but have a particular opening, a particular clearing within which we can develop and expand, and the forms in which we develop—the forms in which we transcend the limitations that initially define ourselves—are always shaped and figured by this original determinacy. The same is true of our initial participation in the reality of intersubjective life. We do not begin as full participants in a fully formed "we," but have, rather, a particular and determinate contact with others that is the arena within which we can establish routes for grasping, posturing ourselves in, and tasting human reality as such. We enter intersubjectivity through becoming familiar with particular others, and these familiars are our originary vision of intersubjectivity, of "who we are." It is our family—our group of familiars—that first defines for us where we fit into intersubjective relations and, consequently, what will count as the values by which "we" must approach the world, by which we must contact reality. Our family defines for us our proper place, and, indeed, the place of propriety—of value—itself.

Typically, it is our parents, our siblings, and perhaps our grandparents (and ourselves, but ambiguously so, inasmuch as we do not start with our own selves as explicit and clearly defined objects of our perception) who constitute our family and thus initially introduce us to, and define for us, the domain of humans. They count as the representatives of that sphere of "other people" to whose judgment we are subject. They are how we become familiar with other people. Each of these judging centers has a history of developing contact, a "take" on things, a more or less coherent narrative about the nature of things, and this "take," this narrative, provides the terms that determine how that person is prepared to recognize—contact—others and how, in turn, that person demands to be recognized. For the child the behavior of her familiars is fundamentally a gesture telling the story of "who we are." What the child develops from this contact with others—the story that she finds told through this behavior—is its structure of memory and expectation for intersubjective life. Through the behavior of these others, the child has impressed upon her the basis for the vision of reality within which she must find her place. The narratives that our family members bring to bear on the situation define the intersubjective parameters in which and through which the child must operate, letting the child know how she will be recognized as properly interpreting her situation. It is through these narratives of recognition that the child is initiated into intersubjective life and these narratives must find a way of being reconciled with each other and with the child's modes of contacting if the child's world is to be coherent and functional. In order to function, these narratives must become the ground of the child's own familiar mode of contact; operating from these narratives amounts to remembering one's place and establishing one's expectations. Such narratives are the intersubjective equivalent of the original determinacies—the hands and the mouth—with which the organic body is born; they provide the fundamental categories—the basic grasps—of intersubjective space by which the child can negotiate her dealings with others and with her own sense of itself. The child, thus, must develop a sense of things—a narrative—that meshes with the way "we" are narrated to her through the behavior of the others.

Upon entering into a family, then, one finds that one can function only if one finds a way to accept a mode of being recognized and of recognizing that integrates with the demands made by the family. (Typically, of course, the parents will hold the ruling position in this power structure, and the narratives of what one's siblings or grandparents will allow will already have had to accommodate themselves to the parental narratives.) The family is the initial sphere of interpersonal life within which we are initiated into a way of recognizing what there is in the world and how our own identity fits within it. As our familiar others, our family members become people from whom we are incapable of separating our own identities. Just as our hands and knees, our height, and our mouths define for us the specific forms our original contacts take, so do our familial others define for us the specific form that our involvement in interpersonal life will take. Just as the later developments of our "I can" will always trace themselves back to the determinacies of our initial bodily involvements, so will our interpersonal identity always carry the traces of our family members as our founding points of human reference. The resources they offer will be as varied as are the resources offered us by our native physiology, and the extent to which they will be inhibiting or enabling will be measured by how sound is the vision of intersubjectivity communicated in the behavioral narratives. Our own analysis has already shown us something of what is really required to account adequately for the existence of a human self, so, to the extent that the familial discourse is at odds with or denies aspects of this account, the developing family member will face tension, and this tension will permeate every relationship into which that person enters, and it will show itself in various domains as a problem, for the person's own existence will lead that person constantly to feel compelled to make certain recognitions that are not recognized by the familial narrative.

Though there are historical situations in which this need not be true, in the modern world the family exists in a social situation contextualized by relations with other people who do not belong to the family (but who belong, of course, to other families). Even as, for each of us, our family defines itself as the definitive sphere of human relations, it also has the function of opening us out onto other human situations. As much, then, as our identities are constitutively defined by a relation with familiar/familial others, our identities are constituted by an opening out onto nonfamiliar others. Emerging as a human subject is, thus, to be initiated into a world defined by a double openness of relations to familiars and relations to strangers. These are the initial axes of intersubjective life.

Strangers do not stay strangers, however. The relations we set up with strangers initiate new forms of relationship that in various ways supersede and override family relations: the very nature of the family is that it opens us to an intersubjective horizon in which who we and our family members are is subject to redefinition (just as the developing of habits that was made possible by our initial bodily openings redefines the significance and nature of those initial bodily openings). Let us consider how this redefinition occurs.

The life of the familiar intersubjective world—the family—involves an establishment of differentiated roles for the various family members: within the family, parents are different kinds of things than children are, and these differences show themselves in the different roles and responsibilities that each considers to be given to it. In particular, we normally think of the successful family as the one in which the parents adopt the role of facilitating

the development of the children to the point that they become independent, self-reliant adults, where this development is achieved by first insisting that the children have their choosing be subordinated to the
decision-making power of the parents. But if what is to happen to the children is that they become self-reliant adults, then part of what growing up
means is precisely discovering that there is not an "ontological" difference
between parents and children, which was the premise of the familial relationship; that is, parents and children are not, in the end, different kinds of
reality, different kinds of being. Rather, the grown-up child recognizes, all
are just free humans with equal capacity to participate in human life, with
the parents simply being former children who appear to their own children
from a position into which those children will themselves develop. (Indeed, our own account of human subjectivity has shown that this is the
narrative of who we are that the family must induce if it is to enable the
family members to live in a way that can be reconciled with itself.)

The very nature of the family, then, is (1) to begin by insisting that
the single individual give over the rights claimed by her singularity for
defining her identity in favor of the right of the particular group to give it
an identity as a particular member, and (2) subsequently to lead by its
own development to an overturning of this notion in favor of a notion of
the universal or commonly shared identity of humankind. The family demands that we replace a sense of the primacy of our singular identity
with a sense of our particular identity within the family; development
within the family, though, demands that this sense of the primacy of our
particular identity be replaced by a sense of the universal identity of
humanity as such. To be born into a family, then, is to be born into the
dualisms of "parents versus children," and "strange versus familiar" ("us
versus them"), but the very enactment of this hold on reality demands
the self-transcendence of this shape of the "I can," that is, it demands the
overturning of these dualisms. In other words, we must come to find our
family members, whom we initially take to be naturally given as special
and necessary (proper), to be strange and contingent, and we must develop *for ourselves* new familiarities with strangers, whom we come to
recognize as legitimately (properly) making demands upon our identities.
The natural trajectory of family life, then, is to overturn its own doubly
dualistic "ontology" or "vision of reality" in favor of a new sort of intersubjectivity governed by the ideal that each participate as a free individual and in which the context is thus defined by the universal identity
and equivalence of humans qua humans.

Social Life

The change within experience from family life to social life—the change from recognizing the family as the primary source of significance to finding the larger, transfamilial social world to be definitive of who we are—can take many forms. In a social world in which participants have only narrow contacts with members of other groups, the sense of what this larger humanity is will be very different than in a world in which there is a broad diversity of human types within the normal social sphere. Consequently, the move from family life to social life can take forms that approximate more to the particularism of the family or more to the universalism of cosmopolitan life. Furthermore, the determinate form the larger social situation takes can itself vary, for different societies can build into their own organization a wide variety of different "narratives" for defining human social life. Consequently, in the case of the larger society, just as in the case of the family and the case of the body, we can see that the determinate form that one's given situation takes will set the limits to the resources that the situation offers for inhibiting or enabling one's development, one's self-transcending activity of contact.

Typically, one is not born into a family simply, but into a family within an already determinate social environment, and the narrative the family enforces through its behavior will have to find a way to reconcile itself with the larger narratives enforced by the society as a whole, just as the narratives of individual family members must fit into the narrative of the overall family power structure if the individuals (the family in the former case, the family members in the latter) are to be able to function. The family is thus both an autonomous form of intersubjective experience and also an agent for initiating the family members into the larger form of social experience. It certainly is true that there can be families that do not function well, and it certainly is true that there can be societies with sufficient complexity or looseness of definition that the precise familial narrative is very far removed from the precise social narrative, but it still must be the case that there be some ground of reconciliation of the family and the larger society if the family is to be able to function within that society that contextualizes it. While there can be extreme variation, then, the logic behind the structure of the family and its relation to society means that it is normally the case that the narrative enacted within familial behavior equally serves to reproduce the larger social narrative. Now, what are these relationships as *phenomena*, that is, how are they figurings of the "I can," of the "making contact"?

How, in other words, do they emerge within the experience of the one growing up?

Typically, one is born into an established community that is going to be the context that is definitive for one's mature identity, that is, we are going to grow up to be independent, adult members of this society. The demand with which one's situation confronts one when growing up, then, is to learn from it who one is going to be by interpreting its portrayal of who we are. This context of other people calls upon one to be a specific sort of person, and learning who one will be is the process of finding a place for oneself within its narrative, which amounts to taking on its traditions while transforming them in a way that allows them to fit one's own new and developing situation. The institutions by which we carry on the memory of who we are and the vision of who we will be— the family first, but others as we become integrated into a larger social life—educate each of us into who each of us is, which means they teach us what there is, how to behave, and so on; in short, they articulate for us the parameters of our human world. But to the one growing up, it is not evident that these are "traditions," "education," "human values," and so on, that is, these are not categories for interpretation with which the child begins. On the contrary, to the child growing up, all such institutionalized, customary behavior can only be taken up as rituals, that is, as demands for compliance that do not first present their own justification. As newly emerged children, we do not generate our social customs from ourselves and we do not see other options, but rather find ourselves in a situation that already operates according to customs—that operates according to particular, already determinate customs. These customs do not explain themselves to us nor do they ask for our consent; on the contrary, it is only by embracing these customs and their implicit narratives that we develop the ability to look for justification and that we earn the right to call upon others to respect our rights, for it is these customs that provide us entry into the intersubjective world in which these issues of justification and respect first become possible.

The world as the new member faces it is a world determinately structured by an intelligibility to which she is not privy, and she must act as a kind of student, asking of her experience how it is that it makes sense. In general, this question amounts to, "How should I act?" and if the child's experienced, intersubjective world is turned to for an answer, it will give an answer, namely, it will say, "act according to the form of our various founding institutions, familial, and social." The new member will find that she is recognized by members of the family and society into which she is born to the extent that her actions conform to their institutions and thereby fulfill their expectations, that is, to the extent that the child animates her actions by the same customs, the same narratives, that animate the behavior of the adults and define for the adults their sense of propriety. Thus the new member becomes an independent person precisely through the process of becoming habituated to a series of intelligent actions the intelligence of which is not explicitly self-conscious to her: her independence comes from relying upon—depending upon—the rightness of the traditions, of the society.

Just as one cannot separate one's identity from the identity of one's family, it is also true, therefore, that one cannot separate one's identity from the identity of one's society, for it is as an appropriation of one's society's narratives that one develops a sense of who one is. It is as a social member that one is someone—that one can be recognized by one's others, and thereby recognize oneself, as someone—and the very capacity that one has to pose the issues of identity and so on is itself a product of participation in that society and its ritual structures of education into human identity. The difference between the phenomenon of the family and the phenomenon of the society is that within the family the familiar narrative into which one was born is automatically decisive, whereas in the society the ruling narrative can override familial narratives and, indeed, has as its particular function the integrating of a multiplicity of families. One's identity in the family is simply one's role as a member—son, mother, and so on—and as a representative agent of the family narrative. One's identity in the society is as a single, equal adult, and as a representative of the transfamilial narrative. To become a member of a larger society, then, requires that one adopt a stance of challenge to the legitimacy of the family narrative. This is the dynamism that we have already seen in recognizing the family as a self-transcending mode of contact.

Participation in the larger society thus entails renouncing the primacy of our immediately familiar intersubjective horizon, that is, it entails renouncing the primacy of the family. To the extent, however, that our participation in the larger society remains a ritual participation, it is still *familiarity as such* that is being privileged in the narrative. To the extent that society advocates adherence to itself *as a traditional society*, the larger society is still basing its human narrative on the logic of family membership, and is thus self-contradictory and reactionary in its mode of making intersubjective contact. Thus the real overturning of family values, the real revolution in social life, comes in the society (or, indeed, the family) that has as its narrative the need to override the authority of familiarity as such. As I noted at the beginning of this section, there can be as many kinds of society as there can be kinds of narrative, and these various types will imitate more nearly the family or the cosmopolis. We have just seen how the traditional society marks the familial extreme of social organization. Now I want simply to articulate the cosmopolitan extreme that marks the most fully fledged social structure, because this will show us the *terminus ad quem* of the development of human self-identity, that is, the form of the inherent goal of the human project of mutual, equal recognition.

What form of contact would this universal society take? What would its narrative be? Basically, its narrative would have to be the very narrative articulated in the preceding pages. It would have to advocate universality for a human population recognized to be creating itself as networks of self-transcending intersubjective contacts from out of specifically figured situations of social familiarity. Our account allows us to see the necessity that human life be structured by specially figured social familiarities, that is, we can understand why it makes sense that each one of us is "embodied" in a specific set of narrative practices, and we can see how these (different) practices are in fact routes by which—and the only routes by which—individuals can develop for themselves both a self-identity and a sense of that self-identity. If this is the human condition, then the society that is universally open to the human condition must be one that accepts this necessity of social diversity as its premise. The "universal" society, then, is one that acknowledges the experiential primacy of cultural pluralism—of narrative pluralism—and sees the universality of any shared human environment as something to be achieved through learning to make such narratives communicate rather than as a given, already existent situation of human equality. The human condition is this given variety of narrative differences. The givenness of this variety, though the starting point for intersubjectivity, is not the finished state of human contact for it is itself—like the body and like the family—a self-transcending situation of openness in that, as we have here seen, the goal of achieving this universality is inherent to the form of every social narrative qua social narrative. The universal human condition is to be a plural situation of cultural narratives, each of which is inherently propelled toward transcending and transforming these given differences through establishing a communication between them.

This means that, experientially, there will always be for us nonfamiliar others, and their practices will seem strange. The very nature of our interpretive contact is to embody itself as habitual structures of intersubjective familiarity, but, since our familiarities will always be particular, determinate, historically, and culturally specific practices, they will always be perspectives that open out onto an outside, onto other determinate practices that are not governed by the same specific, historical rituals. Consequently, our very familiarity with the human world propels us into relations with strangers. What our study shows, though, is that, even though the gestures of others—both as single individuals and as cultural groups—are to us initially empty and puzzling, and do not appear as immediately and obviously demanded by the situation, we must nonetheless recognize that they are such in fact, that is, we know from our analysis of subjectivity that they are how the objectivity of the others' situation makes demands upon them (inasmuch as those others are the living memory of their commitments to specific projects of interpersonal recognition within their ritual society). Furthermore, the ideal of the universal society that is the natural goal of our intersubjective life demands that we must proceed from this experience of strangeness to a recognition of the inherent intelligibility of those foreign practices; or, rather, the phenomenological meaning of "foreign practice" is precisely the demand to be understood. The key to our ability to see this inherent sense of alien practices is precisely our ability to recognize that these gestures are players in the universal human task of seeking mutual recognition and confirmation of identity, and of doing this by jointly inhabiting a world that in its familiarity functions as a confirming mirror for the expectations of normalcy upon which we found our sense of self.

It is from this character of intersubjective life that we can see the basis for the human projects of knowledge and morality. Our very embodiment, as an openness to the demands of making sense, always implicates us in recognizing *on their own terms* the determinacy of others, which, we have seen, ultimately means other people. To be an intersubjective body is to be already implicated in issues of authority, and our study of the path of intersubjective life has shown why it is that we are necessarily beholden to a project of universal answerability, of having our own measuring of significance measure up to the standards of others. Our embodiment is in its very essence a critical, that is to say an interpretive, engagement with determinacy, but it is a critical stance that, by its own intrinsic logic, opens within itself into the domain of answerability to other perspectives, that is, into the domain of rational criteria. The goal of objectivity in knowledge is just this demand to be answerable in one's interpretation of the significance of the world to the ways in which experienced determinacy is open to interpretation of others. The experience of moral obligation is just another perspective on this same experience of the legitimacy of others taking a critical response toward one's own practices.

Opening onto the intersubjective realm is thus opening onto the realm of criticism, of the conflict of interpretive stances. Other individuals and other cultures often have practices of which we are critical, and we can have good reasons for our criticism. The way in which a social custom or any familiar personal practice exists for the perspective of the one criticizing is not, however, the way it exists for the agent who achieves a lived, communal self-confirmation through that practice: first and foremost, familiar practices are ritual structures of intersubjective recognition, and they must be comprehended as such, and not confused with the way they appear as alien and contingent practices within the world of the criticizing ego. Critique is an essential dimension of our intersubjective life as we have already seen: to enter society is the internally anticipated outcome of family life, to enter society is to criticize the family, and to enter the universal society proper is to criticize the primacy of familiarity as such. But because the only route any of us has to meaning is through our figured contacts and their attendant practices, the only form of critique of those contacts that can do justice to the human demands of social, familiar life is "indwelling" critique, that is, criticism must be something that develops from within the terms of the lived social situation—the figured contact—itself. Furthermore, while this necessity that familiar practices be open to their own immanent, self-transcending critique entails that the stance of criticizing others is legitimate, it is also true that we must ourselves embrace the legitimacy of the criticism of ourselves by others on the very same grounds. Intersubjective embodiment entails that we participate in a realm in which the criticism of others and also of ourselves is both possible and necessary.

In chapters 5 and 6 we will see more exactly how this theme of intersubjective critique as immanent self-transcendence appears within human life. We have now sufficiently articulated the drive and direction—the central substance—of the human project in general, and we can turn to the study of the formation of personal identity within this human project, and to its characteristic patterns and problems. Specifically, we will see why human development naturally takes us into that sphere of phenomena typically referred to as "mental illness."

5

Neurosis

Originary Dissociation

We have so far studied the nature of the human project and the form in which it carries itself out as an embodied agency. In part, this study has been an answer to the question, "How did we get here?" where "here" names the typical prejudices of familiar life with which we began our study. Our study has taken us to the point of recognizing why the embodied subject-object contact is motivated to take the form of experiencing itself as a single self in relation to other, equal selves. This development is integral to what we have seen as the emergence of social—suprafamilial—life. This last development, however, can take on a range of different forms, and these forms, again, can be more or less adequate to living up to the intrinsic needs of intersubjective contact. These different forms of contacting the social bring with them different postures of the single self; the self of the typical prejudices that we have been studying is the most basic posture of this self in social contact, and it is a very important and powerful mode of contact. As we have seen through our criticism of these prejudices, however, it is ultimately not a satisfactory stance. We now have to consider more exactly what is its source and power, and what its problem.

In studying this stance of our intersubjective contacting that is so familiar to us—the stance of the "ego"—we will again be discerning the dynamic, self-transcending character of a stance that typically takes itself to be static and settled. We will see how disparity between what it is and what it takes itself to be is the source of significant problems in human life. In studying this posture we will see why human life characteristically faces problems in its development—specifically, we will understand how the development of our subject-object contact becomes a neurotic posture. The material we have so far developed in our study of our interpretive, embodied contact will allow us to understand the problems of human development primarily in terms of the notions of intersubjective recognition, familiarity, and memory.

In the preceding material I have argued that the dynamism of embodied humanity in part involves the progressive attempt to develop (in the context of relations with others) a sense of who one is: "What claims about myself can I maintain?" I have also argued that there is a satisfactory theoretical answer to this question in general, and that is what I have tried to articulate throughout each of these chapters. In other words, our account in this book shows us the basic form that the coherent answer would take to the question we all ask. Consequently, we should not be surprised to find that people who live their lives around an attempt to maintain a different self-definition face problems and incoherencies in their lives. This is what we will now consider: we will see how certain stategies for answering the question of self-identity are problems for the very self that is involved in asking and answering this question.

From what we have seen, we know that our identity begins as a multiplicity. We are a set of figured contacts that are the production of—the performance of—significance (determinacy), and we enact a general propulsion toward bringing the multiple significance that is our experience into a situation of coherence. Our contacts provide us with—define us as—so many local regions of contact, each of which articulates a self-identity and a world. The narratives according to which each of these regional practices operates can, and typically will, conflict with each other to varying degrees. The explicit recognition of the significance of the conflicts of these local systems is itself a relatively late development within the project of cohering. The dynamism of conflict and resolution has, however, an implicit operation as well.

We have pursued this notion of how our contacts are figured—determinate and multiple—in relation to the themes of embodiment and intersubjective relations, and we have seen that moods are the immediacy of how it feels to be determinately embodied. In our habitual, intersubjective involvement with our world, then, we find ourselves immediately open to certain paths and immediately closed to certain others. Being sad, for example, makes (means) certain courses of action feel obvious and available, which implies that others feel closed off and impossible with equal obviousness. Being in such a mood makes some sides of life seem close, others distant, in accordance with the projective commitments of which this emotional behavior is the memory. All mood is thus a form of dissociation. When we are in one mood, we have being revealed to us—revealed in its obviousness—in one way; it is a determinate way, which means we cannot see other ways. When we are angry with someone we cannot remember what it is like to feel tender toward that person, and, similarly, when we again become tender we cannot see how we could ever be angry with that person. We see an intense and pathological version of such dissociation of mood in the familiar scenario of the man who characteristically oscillates between experiencing his wife as someone to be beaten and experiencing her as a vulnerable and dear companion in front of whom he must repent and abase himself. In our different moods, we are, in a basic way, like different selves.

Such dissociation is our original mode of being in a world, and is not a falling away from a prior state of self-unity. It is original, in that it is the condition from which we start, and it is "originary," in that this condition is what makes available to us a determinate contact with the world: it is our creative "reach," our initial capacity for self-transcendence. It is as thus dissociated, as "moody," that we enact any embodied contact, any disporting with significance. Our moods are our ways into meaning, into developing a meaningful situation.

We have seen from our discussions of habit and intersubjectivity that the intelligibility that is the content of our developed moods, the content that is the form they give to a whole situation, is essentially a strategy for intersubjective relations. Different moods are different interpretations of what we face, which means primarily who we are in relation to each other, and this interpretation involves a projection into the future of what should be done. So our moods are how we feel our habitual paths of dealing with others, how these paths are called up for us in and as our objects. Our emotional life in general could thus be construed as the defenses we have constructed in order to cope with the challenges we have faced in our efforts to assert the centrality of the claim that "I matter." The world confronts us with a variety of obstacles, challenges, and assaults, and our emotional life is our developed style for carrying on in the face of such opposition.

Of course, to use the term *defense* shifts the rhetorical weight in the opposite direction from the direction implied by the term *skill*, for example, and it is certainly true that our emotions could equally be called our skills for having a world. The former term rightly conjures up the sense of the oppositional context out of which much of our emotional life is built. The latter term rightly conjures up the sense of agency and singular initiative that makes possible one's emotional life. This latter sense emphasizes the way in which our moods are the ways we have developed for being open to the determinacy of our world. Essentially, our moods are our accomplishment—that of which we can be proud—in the context of opening ourselves to, and defending ourselves against, the interventions of others.

Our moods are our accomplishment of the defense of our self-identity: they are the routes we have found to *being someone* in the face of the demands of the world. As we have just seen, the primary struggle we face in our contacts is establishing a sense of ourselves that our contact will tolerate. The shape that our identity takes is determined by how we carry out this struggle. Though our initial sense may be that "I am everything that matters" we are quickly told the opposite: we are really subject to a huge range of demands we cannot control—things that will not bend to our will, parents who order us around, and so on—and it very quickly seems that we are nothing in the face of a world that seems as if it would get along just fine without us.

Indeed, this experience of being challenged in our sense of the fundamental importance of our own selves is the source of the prejudice of the ontological independence of the object of experience, with which we began our study. This prejudice in favor of the independent reality of the world is described by Simone de Beauvoir in *Ethics of Ambiguity*:

> The child's situation is characterized by finding himself cast into a universe which he has not helped to establish, which has been fashioned without him, and which appears to him as an absolute to which he can only submit. In his eyes, human inventions, words, customs and values are given facts, as inevitable as the sky and the trees. . . . The real world is that of the adults where one is allowed only to respect and obey. (p. 35)

In relation to things in general, but particularly in relation to our family narratives, it is hard for us to establish a sense of our own importance since so much of our upbringing is a demand that we change and be different from the way we automatically are: don't poop in your pants; don't pee on the floor; don't poke your feces; don't pick your nose; don't pick my nose; don't talk when others are talking; don't put your elbows on the table. The child's contact with the world is fundamentally a demand to conform to the authority of its already established ways, its independent reality.

This original familial situation of being challenged to establish "proper" identities for ourselves and others is described by Gilles Deleuze and Félix Guattari in *Anti-Oedipus*:

> The inscription performed by the family follows the pattern of its triangle, by distinguishing what belongs to the family from what

does not. It also cuts inwardly, along the lines of differentiation that form global persons: there's daddy, there's mommy, there you are, and then there's your sister. Cut into the flow of milk here, it's your brother's turn, don't take a crap there, cut into the stream of shit over there. Retention is the primary function of the family: it is a matter of learning what elements of desiring-production the family is going to reject, what it is going to retain. . . . The child feels the task required of him. But what is to be put into the triangle, how are the selections to be made? The father's nose or the mother's ear—will that do, can that be retained, will that constitute a good Oedipal incision? And the bicycle horn? What is part of the family? (p. 125)

family stories

It is through the enforcement of the familial narratives that the child is confronted with the demand to interpret her experience according to the parameters of the "proper identities" of things in the world, despite that fact that in the child's own experience the situation is initially only a wealth of diverse bodily contacts. Acceptance within the intersubjective world that the child experiences with her familiar others requires that the family system supplant the singularity of the child's ambiguous and amorphous situation. To a very great extent our coming to be family members—which requires giving up the privilege we hold out for our singularity and replacing it with a privileging of membership, the terms of which are defined by our elders—is like breaking a wild horse. Cultivation of familial identity largely amounts to establishing prohibitions as a code for what will be inside and what will be outside the realm of propriety, that is, inside or outside the world of "the good," "the proper," and "the real," that is defined by the family.

Our real challenge as we grow is to be recognized as actually being someone—someone who counts within the real world, someone whose being actually makes a difference—by the family that defines for us the real world of value. Once we adopt the view—the view our world demands of us if it is to allow us to advance—that the family sets the standards for reality (= propriety) we find that our struggle is really to establish in their eyes that we are actually someone. It is on these terms that our contact with our world is articulated and developed, and so the habits we develop for figuring our contact are our habits of establishing that we are someone. "How can I count as real in the eyes of those who matter" is the challenge in relation to which we develop strategies and capacities. To the extent that these become familiar and inconspicuous—to the extent that they become habits—they present themselves only as the immediacy of a pervasive memory as promissory mood. In this way, then, our moods are our fundamental achievement of our ability to be someone in the face of our contact with our world.⌡

Our initial way of being someone, qua emotional, is dissociated. We have already seen this with the simple notion of the diversity of moods. In a more extreme way, though, we live as people who constantly face conflicting stories within ourselves about ourselves. In our lives we typically oscillate between differing narratives about ourselves that are more explicit than the pervasive immediacy of simply being-in-a-mood. From different histories of contact we develop different local strategies, systems, practices, and narratives concerning ourselves, those we face, and the world that provides an arena for these exchanges. These local narratives are often at odds with one another regarding who they paint us as being, and so on. These conflicts are often most manifest in the presence of other people, when we find, for example, that a style of behavior that comes easily to us with some companions is not one that we can maintain in front of others. Around some friends, for example, I can be confident, but around another person, perhaps my father, I think of myself as weak and incompetent. Or again, I may live with a sense of myself as an aggressive leader on the basketball court, but treat myself as a timid follower when I shop for clothes with my mother. These differences in self-interpretation are typically and originally simply diverse from domain to domain, but they can be heightened to the point of actual conflict or, indeed, extreme contradiction.⌡

To some degree, such differences can be maintained unproblematically, for there need be no immediate points of contact between one sector of life and another. On the other hand, each local narrative projects the possibility of accounting for everything beyond its horizon, that is, each narrative claims about itself that it is the truth, and therefore impacts upon the others in principle. Even if there is no immediate point of contact between two sectors, they implicitly impact upon each other, for at a fundamental level each realm of contact operates with the view that it is the same "me" acting as in each other case, that is, each of these spheres of local contact rests on the premise that it can be an engagement with the world that coheres with the rest of my contacts. Furthermore, these different local sectors of contact often do get developed to a point at which they do make immediate contact, and it is in such circumstances that the oppositions constitutive of the differing narratives do become heightened to the point of conflict. When we are young, for example, walking, sleeping, and eating may initially seem to be private activities, and quite separate from having friends, yet as we grow older and our friendships develop into an adult form, we find walking, eating, and sleeping are all ways of being with another person, and our ways of navigating these spheres are no longer comfortably private, when, for example, our slow, stately approach to walking sits uncomfortably with the demands of a friendship with a particular person whose style of life relies on quick, aggressive travel, or when one's spouse finds one's sleep routines irritating and inconsiderate. In such situations, we discover that our modes of walking, eating, and sleeping are actually intersubjective gestures, and the other person very much feels how these forms of activity embody our care for herself, just as we directly recognize the way we are being treated by another's habits of walking, eating, and sleeping. Such situations reveal that these sectors of our activity are not in fact separate, as they perhaps first appeared, but each has the other on its horizon as a determinacy to which it must answer. As we develop our lives in each of these spheres they come to intersect with others, and each thereby reveals that it is implicitly subject to the norms of the other. As emotionally and habitually dissociated, we thus automatically live in a state of implicit self-challenge, and this self-challenge can itself come to be explicitly experienced when local contacts develop to the point of intersecting with each other.

This situation of self-dissociation is basic or "natural" to our human condition, but it is also the ground of what is called "neurosis." We call it "neurosis" when this dissociation is a problem, when some sector of a person's life cannot function compatibly with the demands of intersubjective life as developed in other sectors of that person's life. Much more serious than incompatibilities at the periphery of our habits of taste or of polite interaction are conflicts that arise between our most basic habits for dealing with others and the demands that characterize our developed interpersonal affairs, and it is here that we find the most serious neurotic problems.

As a child, a woman encountered an arbitrary and authoritarian father and a mother of unpredictable mood and behavior. The household was a site of consistent discomfort, being characterized by frequent outbursts of anger from her father that included threats, humiliation, hitting, and various forms of invasion of privacy, and milder forms of erratic, oppressive behavior from her mother; furthermore, in such situations of conflict, her parents typically accused her of being the one whose aggressive behavior was responsible for the problem. Psychological "survival" in this context required habits for coping with such pressures. As a child, this woman was motivated by her situation to develop a habit of being constantly alert to the explosion of violence; somewhat like a badger, this girl was peaceful when left on her own, but quick and fierce in response to threatening behavior. She furthermore had to develop the ability to hold onto a sense of her own innocence in the face of unfair accusations of aggression. This girl was introduced to the intersubjective realm as a site governed by the constant threat of unprovoked assault, and, moreover, assault precisely from those whom she was also required to trust and love most intimately as her primary caregivers. Her parents were both those to whom she needed to turn and those from whom she needed to flee, those whose narrative of herself she had to accept and those whose narrative of herself she had to reject. They induced in her a contradictory experience of other persons, and this motivated her to develop self-defensive habits of suspicion and retaliation. Such habits make good sense in her family situation, and it was by developing such skills of interpretation that she was able to negotiate her family environment. In her adult life, however, these habits of human interaction fit poorly with the demands of her important personal relationships. What was wise circumspection in her dealings with her parents is unjustified distrust when turned on her nonoppressive friends and companions. The fierce fighting back she practiced as a child was a legitimate and praiseworthy insistence on her rights and her independence as an autonomous individual; this same practice deployed against her adult friends is an excessively aggressive overreaction to minor conflicts. In most regions of her life, this woman has developed a rich and rewarding interpersonal life, but the slightest suggestion of opposition can trigger in her a set of habits geared toward fighting, and she becomes, as it were, another person, now operating out of the values of suspicion and retaliation that are incompatible with the values of justice and civility that normally govern her dealings with other people. What were praiseworthy skills of self-defense are now problematic forms of unfair aggression. Such dissociation, whereby the woman's situation motivates her to switch compulsively between two incompatible patterns for interacting with others is a substantial neurotic problem, discernible by herself and certainly by those companions who become the unsuspecting targets of her fighting habits.

We can now turn to the analysis of these neurotic, dissociative problems that shape our personalities and inhibit our achievement of happy and healthy lives. Our contemporary cultural narrative offers a system for interpreting such problems: it designates a pattern of contact as neurosis when the sectors of a person's life fall short of developing to the level of the independent, separate self of life in civilized society, that is, it upholds a model of the civilized self as the norm for human development. In fact, however, this latter self—what I will go on to call the "normal" self or the "ego"—is the very self whose prejudices we have been criticizing from the beginning. Accordingly, although, as we shall see, this cultural narrative does tell us something very important about the nature of neurosis, we should also expect that there is a fundamental problem in this typical view of mental illness and its attendant norm of "normalcy." It is to the relation of the neurotic and the normal that we now turn.

Normalcy and Neurosis

Typically in our development we do accept the legitimacy of the narrative that specifies the need to develop beyond the insistence on the primacy of family life to a recognition of the primacy of a superfamilial society. The sense of oneself that accompanies this narrative about the intersubjective world in general is the sense of oneself as an independent, free agent, ontologically equal with all others: what is posited is the ideal of "humanity as such" within which I count as a human. Now this general narrative itself can be interpreted in a number of different specific forms, with respect to both the determinate sense of what the human society as a whole looks like and the determinate sense of what its correlative human members look like. In our Western society at least, the most typical form of this narrative specifies the form of society that is articulated in the various legal codes developed in early modern Europe (themselves based largely on Roman legal codes), which have been used as the foundations for the societies of Western Europe and North America, and the form of individual that I have identified in this study in terms of the prejudice of discrete individuality. This is precisely what I am calling the "normal self of civilized society."

According to this narrative, the self (as we saw in our study of the prejudices of presence in chapter 1) is a discrete individual, separate from a world of things and other individuals upon which she passes judgment, and separate from her own embodiment, which is treated as a tool or a vehicle that she "has" or "uses." The corresponding social order is understood to be the world of explicitly formulated laws that regulate the commerce of such normal selves in order to provide a social environment in which each is free to pursue her own chosen interests (a) without interference from others, provided (b) she does not herself engage in pursuits that interfere with others engaging in their own free pursuits. Now this notion of the free individual self in the free, universal, human society is a very important notion, because it is a challenge to the supremacy of family rule and because it recognizes the irreducibility of the standpoint of the single body. At the same time, for the reasons we have seen in this book so far, it cannot be an adequate narrative of human life for it is built on a conception of the human situation that misrepresents our embodied, intersubjective character. This posture of subjectivity, therefore, points to its own need to be superseded just as it was itself the result of the self-supersession of family life. There is an implicit, self-transcending character to family life and, for the family member, achieving the free selfhood of normal, civil society is the appropriate, immediate goal implicit to its self-transcending character. For this normal self to which it aspires, though, there is in turn a further goal that it inherently and implicitly projects for its own development. For the time being, we can leave consideration of this second (ultimate) goal, and linger with the transition from family member to civilized, normal self.

To become a normal self is to learn about oneself that one can mobilize various powers within oneself to overrule or shut down the demands of certain local sectors, that one can exercise control within one's environment according to one's wishes. I burn my hand, for example, and the primitive habitual interpretation I have developed for such situations is to shout and moan and focus all my attention and the attention of the whole surrounding world on the injured hand. This set of habitual, emotional reflexes, though, impacts upon other sectors of my experience. The injured hand also functions in the world of cooking, with which I am currently in contact. The shouting mouth also functions in the world of friendly discourse with my dinner companions. Here we see that the local narrative attached to my primitive responses to pain at the level of my most immediate organic involvements conflicts with the local narratives attached to cooking and entertaining. These latter narratives interpret my hand as something that needs to continue performing cooking operations and my mouth as something that needs to express polite pleasantries. To be normal is to find that in case of this conflict of narratives one can exercise control over which set of habitual responses triumphs. The normal ego is the self who learns that "I can choose not to scream out in pain, but to endure it and not let it be what dictates to me my attitude." To become a functioning member of civil society requires that one learn how to make such choices about one's behavior. More precisely, one must adopt the value of exercising this control as against the value of operating out of familiar habits: self-control as such—being a chooser—is the central value in the narrative of civil life. It is this that is taken to be the mark of humanity, of "being civilized."

The neuroses, then, mark the incomplete effecting of this transition to normalcy. We call something a neurosis when some sector of a person's behavior stands as a hindrance to achieving this normal selfhood, that is, one finds oneself still burdened by the compulsion of familiar narratives that function in one's life as crippling, inarticulate moods in which one finds oneself launched into patterns of behavior that stand at odds with the patterns one would otherwise choose. To be neurotic is to find that one cannot control one's behavior in areas that, according to the narrative of normalcy, should be areas in which the free ego has an uninhibited ability to exercise choice. In exploring this notion further, we will see that it is the logic of habituation that is the key to understanding neurotic behavior. We will also see how the very existence of neurosis gives the lie to the narrative of the normal self and, indeed, we will come to see how the very posture of normalcy itself is a neurotic posture.

A woman feels that she has to eat. She has a general project in her life of trying only to eat well-balanced meals at regular times, but right now she cannot restrain her desire to buy bags of candy and to eat them all immediately. She cannot understand her behavior: she feels herself simply to be weak and bad, unable to control herself. As a strategy for dealing with this she becomes particularly cruel to herself, refusing herself any tasty food and dwelling on self-condemnatory thoughts. Now, from the point of view of a society and a person who believe that humans are by nature free and independent individuals, that the proper and normal condition for persons is to choose for themselves what they want and to be held personally responsible for their choices, it cannot be plausible to say here that the woman cannot control herself. From the point of view of the ideal of normalcy, one can only say that this woman must have chosen to eat, and that she is at fault: she wanted the candy and she chose it; there is no other place to turn to find the intelligibility of this situation. In her stance of self-condemnation, the woman has adopted this narrative of the normal self of civil life.

This interpretation, however—the interpretation according to the narrative of the normal self of civilized society—is clearly inadequate. The a priori claim that she must have been able to control herself is not accurate as a phenomenological description of her experience. No doubt the woman herself senses this to the extent that she really believes about herself that she *cannot* control her eating, that is, it is not true that she can simply and immediately change her behavior if she so desires. We can understand why this is so if we reflect back on what we have already learned in our study.

Our study of embodiment has revealed that our capacities for developed action, and specifically our capacity to account for our own identity, are themselves only available to us on the basis of the habitual relationships we have accomplished. It is true that we are beings who are capable of choosing and thinking and being self-reflective, but these are capacities that we must accomplish: they are not given, but developed. The woman who is troubled by her eating is therefore misdirected and unfair to herself in chastising herself for her uncontrollable eating. She acts as if bringing about a situation of control is simply an available option she failed to take and as if inflicting pain upon her putative choosing self will get that self to choose differently next time. In fact, however, the choice was never simply and immediately in her power: being able to control oneself is not something one can presume, for this ability is not given but achieved. The woman's strategy of punishing herself and hoping that she will control herself better thus misses the mark, because it does not address the real source of her actions: developing the ability to control herself will not come through putting pressure on her immediately self-present, reflective ego, but will instead come through a strategy of reeducating her habits. Rather than punishing her choosing ego for choosing wrongly, she must instead study her actions to understand how her habitual self is enacting intelligent patterns of behavior in response to the call of familiar situations.

Now it is not familiarity and habits that are to be done away with in order to fulfill human life in a life of self-conscious freedom. On the contrary, our analysis has shown us that our very identity is inescapably built out of habits, and this will always be so. It is rather the prejudice in favor of the primacy of familiarity that has to supersede itself. The prejudice of familiarity insists that things are good—are "to be done"—simply because they are habitual; it is this value that must be superseded with a value of intelligent choice. We will develop ourselves as freely self-conscious not by getting rid of habits, but by developing the habits of contact that support us as choosers. Primarily, these are habits of understanding, which are themselves habits achieved through the practice of explicit articulation, of rendering explicit and mediated what initially appears opaque and immediate. By the time we are adults it is very likely that we will have developed some of the habits of articulation and expression that do allow us to behave as intelligent choosers, which means that to some extent we will be able to control ourselves; but since it is because of these habits that we can do this, if the habits are primitive, incomplete, or unrefined so will be the practice of choosing.

If the woman of the previous example wants to change, it is her habits that will have to change. If she is to make a plan to effect these changes (and making such changes is typically a long-term and difficult project) it will not do to base the plan on the self-interpretation described in the example; on the contrary she will have to come to understand her behavior as itself rooted in habitual patterns of contact that have their own reason for being. It is the habits she has developed in her life for coping with her intersubjective world—mostly the world of her family within which arena her identity as a person was fought out—that have allowed her to accomplish the self-identity she currently lives. Much as her habit of eating runs contrary to the demands of her current life, it remains true that that habit has been instrumental in making her the person who can have the life she currently has (a consideration of how such a habit can be constructive will be the subject of the last section of this chapter). She cannot successfully engage with that habit without understanding what it is, which means that if she wants to have an ability to change that part of her personality she must come to understand that part of herself, which means learning how it is an habitual, intelligent response to certain types of situation. She must see that her neurotic compulsion is really a habit that was a good habit in a former (formative) context of intersubjective contact but one that is out of joint with the demands of her current situation. Her behavior enacts a memory—or rather, it is the memory—of who she is, but it is out of step with the self she has become. Her memory is a remembering of originary events—self-transcending, creative strategies for making contact—but it remembers them as static inasmuch as these strategies are no longer living, interactive strategies whose viability is under debate; rather, they are fixed habits. Furthermore, these are strategies based on narratives—interpretations—of her situation that other sectors of her life have superseded, but that have not themselves been superseded on their own terms, that is, in their local terrain. To eat is to remember a certain self, a certain "I can" of intersubjectivity, that is "behind the times" of her current intersubjective reality. Because the habit is a habit of interpretation, changing her habit will mean building new habits *of interpretation* that will supersede her old ways. But since her very capacities for intelligence and interpretation are embodied in her habits, this learning will mean working with the capacities afforded by the old habits to change those very habits. Her goal must become rehabituation that means she must want not to act in specific ways simply because they are familiar, but to become familiar with the specific ways she wants to act.

Developing the habits of freedom (which ultimately means habits of mutual recognition) is the goal intrinsic to our self-transcending, embodied, moody intersubjectivity. Habituality is our nature, but the very habits we have developed in order to become adults are habits for analysis, synthesis, imagination, and interpretation. Our habits are the habits of coming to be able to recognize the complexities of the determinacies that characterize our contacts. We cannot escape being creatures of habit—and there is no reason to want to—but the very development of those habits should lead us to understand the need to challenge the givenness of our specific habits, and their attendant conservative, ritualistic character.

Developing the ideal of normalcy definitely marks an advance in the person, for it marks the recognition of the problem of familiarity along with the goal of freedom. To live according to a "normal" persona, then, is a mark of adulthood, as compared with the persona of "family member," which means essentially the persona of slave or child (i.e., one to whom rules are dictated and who must know her naturally assigned proper place of subordination to the rulers of the family and to the institution of the family as such). The stance of normalcy is nonetheless inadequate according to the picture of humanity we have so far developed, however, and it is also inadequate according to its own values, as we can see if we bring the phenomenon of normal selfhood to clearer focus.

The ideal of normalcy pictures a self that is calm, cool, and collected—a self that is not immediately swept away by circumstances, but can endure the experience of various conflicting passions and can stand back in dispassionate contemplation of the situation and control its own decisions and actions. The normal self of civilized life is pictured as a self-contained choosing power that is not intrinsically compelled by its body, by its emotions, or by its family ties: these latter aspects can be subjects about which the normal self makes choices, but they cannot control its very choosing ability. To hold the normal self as an ideal is to hold this notion of independent choice as the primary value in human existence.

This ideal denies the worth of immediately felt values in favor of the worth of detached, reflective consideration. The ideal of the normal self holds as primary the value of our deliberate choosing, which means that it sets itself up as an opponent to a life shaped and governed by emotion. Just as the normal self sets itself in opposition to the familial self, so too does it set itself against the life of emotion.

This denial of the place of feeling, however, is ultimately incoherent. The stance of normalcy intends to get beyond being governed by emotion, but in truth it is a position that simply elevates one passion to a position of tyranny within its decision making. The appearance of dispassionate self-control in the normal self really rests on the fact that a brand of cruelty or self-hatred has become, in the normal self, the ruling passion. The normal self feels successful when she can overcome the immediate feeling that presents itself. The normal self wants to eat a treat, but does not—and feels virtuous for making a wise diet choice. The normal self wants to explode in anger at the boss, but does not—and feels responsible and professional for not letting emotions cloud the issues. The normal self feels like expressing embarrassment or excitement, but does not—and is proud of her cool appearance. The normal self feels like crying, but does not—and is proud of her stoic resolve. In each case, the successful maintenance of the posture of normalcy amounts to a stance of self-denial, and it is from this successful self-denial that the normal self derives pleasure; it is in such self-denial that the normal self finds worth.

There is an anecdote told about the city of Minneapolis, a city whose residents are reputed to be excessively stoic, and this anecdote captures well the notion of stoic self-denial that lies implicit in the ideal of normalcy. According to the joke, an elderly resident was said to love his wife so much that he almost told her so before he died. This remark expresses well the essence of stoicism as a mode of intersubjective contact. The stoic is the person who has made a virtue out of renouncing the immediacy of contact, of vulnerability, and has come to define herself as a locus of self-control and choice that holds itself in reserve from embodiment and living engagement. The stoic has sealed herself off from others with a defensive wall of silence and refusal. This defensive sealing up of oneself—this withdrawal from others, from emotion, and from embodiment—is just the extreme end of the ideal of normalcy, for the values of stoicism and the values of normalcy are at root the same.

The driving value behind stoicism and normalcy is the value of detached choice—choice detached from the taint of the specificities of bodily, emotional, intersubjective life—and this value goes hand in hand with a vision of human existence according to which the power of choice is simply given to us as already fully within our control. Our own study in this book so far, however, has given the lie to this picture of human life. We have seen, on the contrary, that the very specificities from which normalcy would have us withdraw are in fact the very substance of our reality. The ideal of the normal self is an ideal of singular isolation, but we have seen that our singular existence is never won in isolation but is, rather, won only through participation and absorption in our surroundings. Our inescapable nature is to be outwardly directed, whereas the ideal of normalcy portrays us as inherently inward. To uphold this value of normalcy, of isolated inwardness, is thus to reject the value of those aspects of ourselves that are our true substance and foundation. To advocate normalcy is to renounce our own humanity. It is in this sense, then, that the value of normalcy is premised on a kind of self-abuse, on a developed sense of dislike and distaste for one's own materiality. As we have already seen, it is our outwardly directed materiality that lets our existence be meaningful to us precisely to the extent that it makes us vulnerable to our outside; the denial of this in the name of normalcy is thus really a defensive refusal of the vulnerability that comes with determinateness, and is thus simultaneously a renunciation of ourselves and of our world. Not surprisingly, a society premised on the narrative of normalcy produces a "civil" society of people alienated from themselves and from each other.

As the stance that takes pleasure in self-denial, then, the stance of normalcy realizes a particular passion—a passion for self-abuse—and in the normal life, this passion is satisfied to the detriment of the other sectors of emotional life. We can now see the truth of what was said above: stoic normalcy itself is the stance of neurosis par excellence, for it is a mode of contact in which one sector of emotional life functions in a way that is crippling to the other sectors. I say the mode "par excellence" because here the hindering emotion is not a periodic threat to the smooth functioning of the core of self-identity but is that core itself.

As a stance of defense against the family, by which one is for the first time able to be someone individual, the ideal of normalcy marks a significant—perhaps the most significant—achievement within human development. It is liberatory to the extent that it puts one for the first time into the position of explicitly addressing the issue of value and choice within human contact. The narrative of normalcy and its attendant vision of selfhood marks the decisive transcendence of the narrative of familial life, and therefore marks the decisive advance into free human development. As a self-hating, withdrawn, close-mouthed stubbornness, however, the stance of normalcy with its prejudices regarding selfhood, embodiment, the world, and other people is a major impediment to subsequent human development. This ideal of the normal self—presumed in much "liberal" political theory—is ultimately oppressive in its political and social implications, in that it is premised on the implicit refusal to acknowledge the inherent embeddedness of the self in its others, and therefore resists both the cosmopolitan ideal that is on the horizon of all human development and is intolerant in principle of the determinacies of other lives that lead others to be other than "normal."

The ideal of normalcy is an advance because it raises the question of choice and individuality within human experience. At the same time, the way it raises these themes is inadequate to the human situation, which means that a program of action designed around this ideal must necessarily run afoul of the human situation. In particular, this ideal leads us to make value judgments about ourselves that are rooted in values of self-abuse: this is a value that turns us against ourselves in largely unhealthy, unproductive ways. It also leads us to misrepresent and misunderstand the causal powers within our situation, with the result that our decision making becomes inefficacious. This ideal introduces the goal of free choice, but does not itself supply the means to realize this goal. Its reach exceeds its grasp, so to speak, and therefore it represents a losing strategy for dealing with our human lot.

The neuroses generally fall within that category of phenomena loosely referred to as "mental illness." We have defined the neuroses as hindrances to the normal life, but also defined the normal life as itself the hindering neurosis par excellence. If the ideal of the normal life is thus tainted, is there any sense then in which we can still speak of the neuroses as a problem, that is, is there a criterion other than normalcy to which we can turn to evaluate the worth of neurotic behavior patterns? Given our account of the human condition, can we still operate with a notion of mental illness, and where does this leave our account of neurosis?

Given the analysis we have so far offered, it is clear that *illness* cannot be used to designate these neurotic phenomena at all if by that term is meant the intervention into an originally healthy life by some alien agent (like a bacterium). It also cannot designate the presence of human features that are "objectively bad" or "unnatural" or "inherently evil," as if there were some external criterion (e.g., normalcy) to which one could turn to determine value. Our entire analysis of the human situation as interpretive and embodied has shown us that meaning can only be an achievement of embodied intersubjective contact, and the significance "ill" can only be a specification of the "I can" of this contact. This means that whatever the significance this—or any—term will have, that significance will have to be generated from criteria internal to the human situation under consideration. Thus, if there is any sense in which these phenomena can be called "ill," the criteria for so assessing them, and the significance of that term, must come from within the phenomena under consideration themselves.

If we stick to the need for an internal criterion of meaningfulness, we can find two related senses in which the notion of "illness" can be applied to neurotic phenomena. First, we can speak of "illness" when the person herself—for example, the woman in our example of eating—has things in her life that announce the conflict, and the possibility of improvement requires her to recognize this as a problem, that is, the person herself finds that she has patterns of behavior that interfere with the successful functioning of her life that she cannot immediately control. The second, related sense in which we can speak of the illness is as the self-destructive self-conflict within the habitual life of the person that is manifest in that person's behavior even if it is not explicitly recognized by that person, evident, perhaps, in the suspicious and aggressive woman with whom this chapter began, a woman whose injured contact with trust—and trust precisely in the context of negative characterizations of herself—may fundamentally inhibit her ability to trust the interpretation of herself as mistreating others. *Illness*, then, is a term that applies to these phenomena only to the extent that it marks out an experience of distress or a discernible logical and behavioral conflict within the different spheres of contact; in other words, it is by the implicit or explicit standards of the situation of contact itself that the behavior is a problem.

In this sense, then, it is always a human situation—and not a normal ego—that is neurotic. The neuroses are the ways in which a multiply figured situation of contact is at odds with itself, such that its inherent trajectory toward freedom is inhibited by its habitual realization of its potentiality. I want to go on to discuss concretely some such neurotic situations, but first I want to discuss the extreme end of this notion of illness as here outlined.

Typically there is a further kind of "mental illness" distinguished from neurosis, and, indeed, it is often thought to be more properly labeled a "mental" or "cognitive" disorder as opposed to the neuroses, which are deemed "emotional" or "affective" disorders. This further phenomenon is psychosis. The psychotic is called "insane"—unsound and unhealthy—because reality for that person does not present a coherent face. For the neurotic patient, the "stoic" core of self-identity and the attendant ability to function "normally" within society remains intact, and the "emotional disorder" is experienced as a disorder and as contained within a specific sector of life. For the psychotic, on the other hand, there is no secure base of self or world in relation to which some piece of behavior could be marked out as appropriate or inappropriate, ordered or disordered, normal or abnormal. To the outside observer, the psychotic individual appears to suffer from an impairment sufficient to interfere grossly with that person's capacity to meet what are deemed the ordinary demands of normal life. The neurotic, in short, seems to suffer from uncontrollable feelings, whereas the psychotic seems unable to think straight.

From the point of view of our analysis, however, we can see that there is no reason to dualize these two kinds of "mental illness." Our account, on the contrary, suggests that the latter, psychosis, is just a more extreme version of the former. The neuroses mark the inability to coordinate the sectors of habitual life coherently, and psychosis is this same problem now shifted to the very core of self-identity. For the neurotic stoic—the normal self—one sector (the emotional narrative of defensive self-abuse and withdrawal) maintains a coordinating and centralizing role within the person, allowing a criterion for evaluation, planning, choosing, and so on. For the psychotic, this one sector is no more privileged than the others. Indeed, this psychosis is just the completed fulfillment of normalcy's challenge to familiarity, for now the familiar comfort of self-restraint and self-abuse offers no more security than any other habitual path for establishing intersubjective contact. The psychotic, we might say, has implicitly recognized the unconvincing character of the ideal of normalcy, but has done this in such a way as to have no criterion for coherence; psychosis is thus a dissociation so extreme that there are no coherent "selves"—no coherent, habitual, emotional identities—in which one can rest, no posture that is not already undermined by the appearance of an equally legitimate, but opposed posture that can be adopted in its stead.

"Mental illness," then, is just the name for the various ways in which the inherent and inescapable multiplicity of our figured, intersubjective situation of contact can come into conflict with itself as it develops. This "illness" does not mark a falling away from our true nature, but refers, rather, to the necessary form all of our lives take to a greater or lesser degree. Our situation—our posture—is inherently neurotic, and the challenge to us is thus to be free within the openings we are afforded by our neuroses—by our determinateness—rather than to be free from them. With this conceptual orientation to neurotic phenomena in place, we can now consider some characteristic forms of neurotic situations.

Neurotic Situations

Through our study we have understood the parameters relevant to making sense of neurotic behavior. Neurosis will be a way of intersubjective interpretation that is itself a memorial, bodily comportment, primarily realized as a way of having a world of objects—a place, a home. Neurosis is experiencing a determinate world as the lived demand to behave bodily in ways that cripple a personality in its efforts to realize itself as an integral, coherent agency where the determinacy of this world is itself the congealed memory of patterns of intersubjective recognition—specifically, the memory of family life, that is, the memory of those patterns of recognition through which, and as which, we were made familiar with other people.

Because neurotic problems are problems located at the core of our sense of ourselves, it is not surprising that these problems are reflected through the most central structures of our embodiment, such as walking, eating, urinating, sleeping, and speaking. Let us consider some of these examples, beginning with walking.

Walking is one of our most basic ways of expressing or enacting our posture as independent agents. We are not born walking, but must learn how to control and coordinate our bodies in separation from, but in cooperation with, the larger environment. This control of the "physical" environment is also very much an issue of interpersonal navigation. Walking gives the child a new degree of participation in the household: there is an equalizing of status between child and others, there is a winning of approval, and the magnified sense of bodily reach is thus equally a magnified interpersonal reach, for the new developments of bodily skill go hand in hand with new developments in what one is "allowed" to do. By developing the upright posture as a relief from various experienced frustrations, the child "takes a step" beyond her identity as a child, and takes a stand in what is recognized as a higher stage of the human world (and, indeed, note our preference for the metaphor of "height" to portray what is better). We become habituated to this upright posture and independent mobility to such a degree that we accept it as our natural way of being, and, indeed, become agents of the reproduction of this value when we in turn evaluate others by this standard of uprightness.

Since to walk is not just a private affair, but is something demanded of us if we are to participate in developed social life, it is not surprising that there should be large interpersonal stakes involved—large issues of self-esteem. That parents desire so much for their child to "take her first step" attests to the great investment in the value of walking that we continue to have into adulthood; the cultural value placed on walking and uprightness as a mark of humanity—perhaps epitomized in the ideal of the runway model or of the marching soldier—is also evident in the sense we often have that those who slouch are lazy or ignorant, or, more prominently, in the problems of self-esteem that are often felt by those whose legs are disabled, or, indeed, by the lower esteem in which others often hold such people. It is easy to imagine a simple neurotic engagement with walking: as we walk, we may feel publicly on display and, under the presumed eyes of others, we may suddenly find that we cannot walk smoothly. A more serious problem has been noticed by some survivors of concentration camps from the Second World War: as they walk, they find themselves compelled to stop and look behind them. Our walking embodies our lived comportment toward the intersubjective world, and it can easily be as problems of walking that we live a troubled intersubjectivity.

Notice, too, that these two problems of walking that I have identified are both experienced as responses to a world, a response to the demands of the objective form of a place. In walking we propel ourselves forward with and against the ground. It is precisely how we actualize the possibilities for development within the spatial environment. We direct ourselves, (re-)place ourselves, and move ourselves according to the terms that the ground and the atmosphere offer. We experience other locations, "there," as drawing or repelling us—the grass may seem inviting, a large open space may seem to require a faster pace—and we choose our route according to cues from the ground that suggest "walk here," "hurry up here," and so on. When the gaze of others is experienced as a loss of control of our gait, we experience the environment as "hard to walk in"; we experience the atmosphere as having causal effects on our behavior. Similarly for the concentration camp survivor, the very nature of the ground is experienced as a place where others can be too, including especially, of course, oppressive others: the very ground they walk on, the place in which they move, elicits the act of looking over one's back as a response that answers to the form of the situation. In walking, we enact one of our most basic ways of embodying our recognition of the demands of our places. Our places, similarly, are the most primitive repositories of our memories, our memories themselves being the real ground of our-selves, that from which, on the basis of which, with which, and against which we must step forth into our social relationships, our future, and our self-identity. Walking, then, is one of our most basic comportments as single, en-worlded selves, remembering and interpreting, stepping for-ward, in place. We can continue this consideration of the memorial, bodily, and intersubjective structures of our situatedness in the example of sleeping.

We tend to think of walking as something just automatic and nat-ural; we forget that we had to learn how to walk and that walking in-volves a very deliberate and active stance on our parts. This presumption of "givenness" is true of our attitude toward sleeping probably to an even greater degree. We think of sleep as something we undergo, not some-thing we do. Obviously, to some extent this is true inasmuch as sleep is the letting go of our immediate agency. But this letting go involves a sig-nificant degree of agency and commitment nonetheless. Our different situations involve different relations of activity and passivity, and sleep has its own distinctive version of this.

• Like walking, sleeping draws attention to our privacy, the singular-ized character of our existence. Unlike walking, however, which is an ac-tivity of putting our singularity forward into the world, and reshaping our situation according to our singular agency, sleeping is a withdrawal of this singular agency; it is leaving the world to carry on without the delib-erate input of ourselves. Since it has this discernable significance, we should see that it is, then, still a response to the world, and it is experi-enced as such: it is a handing over of the reins, so to speak, to the world, with the expectation that one can pick the reins up again upon reawak-ening. Sleeping is thus an interpretation, a gesture, and a recognition: to sleep is to recognize the world as a reliable place, to trust it.

• A neurotic inability to sleep is therefore a plausible response to a world that is not remembered in the form of "trustworthy." To be unable to sleep is to be unable to rest, to have a situation in which shutting down is not acceptable, not safe, which suggests that what is missing in the person's world is a basic context of trust: to sleep would be to let down one's guard, and guarding is only an issue in a world that has a threatening form. A woman who has been a victim of rape and a victim of incestuous advances by her father finds that she cannot sleep; furthermore, despite a strong desire to confide in others about her difficulty, she finds herself afraid to talk about this, afraid to admit to the problem. Both problems—of sleeping and of speaking about it—can be seen as memorial practices, as ways of remembering that "they will take advantage of vulnerability": she lives out the interpretation of the world as one in which one must not show weakness; one must not trust one's situation. The importance of this trust is further shown by her simultaneous desire to share this experience through talking and, indeed, by the fact that she can sleep in the company of close friends. Indeed, the confiding can be an ambivalent flirtation, a gesture toward a sexual intimacy that is, for the woman, a confused emblem of both trust and betrayal. While such a problem of trust need not be manifested as a problem of sleep, it is understandable why sleep as such or the bed in particular is the site at which this neurotic problem manifests itself (this can be true even if, indeed, the originating traumatic experiences have no connection with specific historical incidents of sleeping).

While sleep requires some attitude of compliance or assent from the sleeper, it is not simply a voluntary activity, but is part of the inherent rhythm of bodily, organic life. Sleeping enacts and expresses the inherent vulnerability of our embodiment, the inherent implication of our bodily lives in the lives—in the power—of others (hence, also, the neurotic fear that one will die in one's sleep). In sleeping, the body's openness surfaces, and this organic comportment is the primitive sketch, the primitive figuring, of that openness in which all our intersubjective life is conducted. The bodily vulnerability that is put on display in sleep is an entry into the world of intersubjective trust. Thus, while sleeping has its roots in organic functioning, sleeping becomes a gesture of intersubjective life. This too is why it is intersubjective transformations, rather than organic treatments, that can improve the person's sleeping problem: while the neurotic problem is situated in an organic process, it is a problem that is relieved by being in the presence of a friend. Here again, too, we see how it is our situation—our place, and the objects that comprise it—that carry the significance to which we respond interpretively through our behavior.

While walking and sleeping both seem initially to be phenomena of physiology or organic life, we have seen that they are not phenomena that can be detached from the larger existential and especially intersubjective dimensions of our human life. It is in these bodily practices and as these bodily practices that we interpret, remember, and engage our social world, our human environment. We therefore have been able to understand why the shape of our intersubjective life manifests itself in the forms in which we live out our most primitive bodily practices. These same correlations are visible in neurotic patterns of eating.

Like sleeping, eating draws attention to the body's inherent vulnerability, its dependency upon its environment for its continued existence. Eating is a more active practice than sleeping, inasmuch as in eating the successful response to this "weakness" of the body is not realized involuntarily, but requires the agency of foraging, chewing, swallowing, and so on: eating does not just "come over us" as does sleep. Eating requires a greater effort, and also a more determinate interaction with the surrounding environment than does sleep. Psychoanalysis has drawn attention to the complicated issues of dependency and trust that are associated with the child's early experiences of breast-feeding, and we can see how such issues are elaborated in many of the typical patterns of continuing family life.

Meals are often charged sites for specifically familial interactions, whether at the breakfast table or at the Thanksgiving dinner. In human cultures generally, and especially in modern Western family life, eating is a heavily organized and ritualized process. Anthropologists, for example, have drawn attention to the ways in which cultures rely upon eating rituals to mark the difference between the human world and the animal world: in eating cooked rather than raw foods, we demonstrate our distinction from animals, and for this reason our sense of self-identity is deeply embedded in the status of our eating practices. As we saw in the case of walking, then, so too do we see in eating the tremendous cultural investment in the values of proper eating practices. Within the traditional, extended family, regular or festive meals can be important occasions for demonstrating loyalty to the family or even for carrying out other complicated rituals of bonding, quarreling, resolving disputes, making business arrangements, and so on. We can see a carrying on of a modified sense of this importance of "breaking bread together" in such contemporary practices as business luncheons and political dinners; indeed, "sharing bread" is the etymological sense behind our words *company* and *companion*. Within the modern nuclear family especially, we can see how much can be invested in the habit of collective eating. Teaching children "proper table manners" is deemed an important stage of education for participation in civil society, and parents often have their own pride at stake in developing within their children the patterns of eating behavior that the children will take with them into other social settings. The family meal is also often the privileged occasion for bringing the family together as a unit, in order to reassert its unity in a social world that requires of the parents and the children that they conduct most of their daily activities in independence of each other at the workplace or in school. Our sense of ourselves as human, our sense of cultural identity, and our sense of familial identity are all typically invested in these primitive bodily practices of ingestion. Thus, as the child grows, she finds her developing eating habits to be privileged points of entry into some of the most charged domains of developed intersubjective life.

The dinner table can thus be a primary site for the production or reproduction of family order. As a ritual of family membership, eating dinner becomes the space in which one is defined as doing well or poorly as a family member, and, inasmuch as our familial involvements are our primary initiation into the human, intersubjective sphere, eating can become the privileged space for determining whether one is doing well or poorly as a person. Eating, thus, can take on the meaning of being the, or at least a, primary mode of intersubjective action. Let us consider what eating can mean, that is, how it can be an interpretation, a memorial gesture, and a transformative human action, and how, therefore, it can assume a neurotic shape.

Eating is in part an activity of acceptance, a taking of something into oneself. To participate in eating can be a gesture toward this acceptance: "I can take it." This could have the sense of embrace ("I welcome it in"); it could have the sense of strength ("I can take it all"); it could have the sense of endurance ("I can get it out of sight"). Correspondingly, one can see how vomiting—another seemingly physiological phenomenon—can be in truth an intersubjective gesture of rejection, of rebellion, of a request for help, of a sense of self-incapacity, of inadequacy, and so on: "I can't take (it) anymore." As the site of individualized pleasure, eating can be an activity to which one retreats to become free from stress, or equally an activity in which one feels one's inability to be in a state of self-control. As activity and accomplishment, eating can be a proof of one's success and efficacy in situations in which one is otherwise powerless. And, of course, once one learns of the causal relation between eating, health, and weight, eating can be primarily significant as a way of comporting oneself toward one's appearance or even existence.

These remarks suggest various ways in which the activity of eating can be a sketch of the dimensions of our more developed intersubjective life. We can see how the typical familial context of eating can engage these self-transcending significances of eating. At the dinner table, what one is taking in need not be simply food: if the rules of family life are being served, participating in eating can be the way one "takes in" these familial structures. One swallows the demands made upon one by one's father, one chews on a criticism; if one cannot leave the dinner table until one has cleaned one's plate, then completing the eating is synonymous with freedom from the intersubjective setting. In such a setting it is clear how this activity of eating can be the figure for our developed dealings with family members, with criticism, with propriety, with willpower, and so on. It is in and as these bodily practices and the environments with which they interact that our memories of familial reality are primarily realized. Our family life, which is our entry into the intersubjective, is remembered by us as the breakfast table, the plate of food, the dining area, the feeling of chewing, the upset stomach, and the taste of milk. Conflicts within our intersubjective dealings—within our sense of self-identity—can consequently find a welcome site for enactment in the form of neurotic symptoms within these bodily practices, within these ways of being in place, that are the embodiment, the memory, and the realization of our intersubjective dealings.

A man, for example, wants to lose weight. Losing weight, he believes, will make him more socially appealing. He finds, however, that, despite great accomplishments in other areas of this life, he cannot control his eating, and cannot stick to his project of dieting. The process of losing weight is long and slow, and requires patience and commitment. While he has tremendous initiative for such a project in general, as for many other important projects in his life, he finds that in the long lonely evening hours that he turns to eating, thereby undermining his endeavor.

In his young family life, he was offered little autonomy, little room to shape his own activities and to discover the pleasure of success through enacting his own initiative. Furthermore, he was constantly portrayed by his parents as failing to meet their expectations. At the dinner table, however, he was able to respond to both of these tensions in his experience. First, he could do well, eating as he was told, always completing the task of eating what was served to him; this sense of success was reinforced by the pleasure of eating, which contrasts with the unpleasant feelings associated with work activities at which his parents deemed him unsuccessful, as well as by the sense that this was something he could do privately, inasmuch as he need only answer to himself to determine what did and did not speak to his own pleasures. In particular, the sense of this private pleasure—being able to "pleasure himself" through eating—is a sense of freedom from the injustice of his parents' unreasonable demands. In discovering the pleasure of eating, he discovers a realm outside the family—a realm of free pleasure, of a free sense of himself as independently important. In this way, eating becomes an important arena for his experience of himself as an independent agent.

It is through this familial crucible that this man's sense of what it is to engage in a project was figured. This is true both of his sense (1) of what it is to have a project imposed upon one and to be judged regarding its successful completion and of his sense (2) of what it is to be free and independent in relation to the unfair demands and unjust judgments of others. It is through eating that the concepts of "project" and "freedom" are distinctively figured for him.

Subsequently, to engage in a project is to remember his family, to remember their challenges to his sense of competence. In the course of pursuing a project, these memories are experienced as a gloomy pessimistic coloring the world, from which relief can be found in the activity of eating, itself the memory of pleasurable, successful accomplishment. To be subject to the demands of a project brings with it the sense of unfair imposition and unjust judgment, from which relief is felt—propriety and justice is enacted—through rebelling against the imposition and caring for himself through taking free pleasure in eating, even in a context in which the projects are in fact no longer unjust impositions of unfair parents but are his own freely chosen objectives. For this man, relying on the activity of eating is integral to his very sense of what it is to be happy in the context of carrying out a project, and, consequently, the project of changing his eating has a latent contradiction built into it. The natural form of carrying out his project of dieting will exactly compel him to rely upon eating to deal with the mood that the engagement with a project itself induces, that is, to succeed at carrying out the project he needs to engage in the very activity that it is his project to refuse. And, indeed, in facing this frustrating compulsion to eat he experiences himself as incompetent, which itself pushes him only more strongly to turn to eating to address this feeling. This is a typical bind of neurosis: the very attempt to solve the neurotic problem triggers the neurotic behavior. Here, the

eating is called up as a solution to a particular stress, a way to reaffirm his
sense of his own competence, yet the activity cannot even perform this,
its memorial function, because the terms of the present situation make
this act of eating itself a failure of competence: he is propelled further
and further into his need to eat, exactly as the activity becomes less and
less capable of solving his problem and indeed makes his situation worse.
And, of course, inasmuch as he has identified his weight with his social
incompetence, the sense of incompetence produced by his failure to control his eating likewise reinforces his sense of himself as a social failure
since his weight remains unchanged.

For this man, then, eating has become one of the fundamental
memorial practices that comprises his participation in social life, and it is
the site for, and the embodiment of, his experiences of tensions and contradictions within his intersubjective life, that is, within his grip on how
to integrate his sense of himself with his sense of others. The food, the setting, and the activities of the mouth are the memory of his self-identity. It
is in the experience of chewing, in the tasting, that his familiar sense of
himself is accomplished, that he feels, in his muscles and in his taste
buds, the return of the atmosphere of propriety and justice. And it is as a
compulsion to eat that this lived sense of how he is defined in relation to
others is enacted. From others he wants pleasure and recognition—he is
literally starving for it—but he presumes they will not give it and so he
feels compelled to turn away from the behavior they seek (his modera-
tion in eating and the improvement of his appearance) in order to take
what satisfaction he can privately, both desiring and rejecting the com-
panionship of others simultaneously.

We have seen how such seemingly "physical" practices as walking,
sleeping, and eating are, for us, behaviors that open us onto the human
world of interpersonal recognition and esteem. Sleeping engages interpersonal trust and intimacy; walking elevates us to equality of stature
with others and lets us participate in the world of work and culture. Eating is typically a route into the rituals of responsibility and the transmis-
sion of cultural traditions—manners—and, as with the other actions,
personal self-control in the eyes of others. Through our engagements
with our familial others we find these practices of walking, sleeping, and
eating to be invested with the most basic values that structure intersubjective life. These "humble" origins to our humanity are present, too, in another seemingly "natural" practice, namely, the excreting of bodily wastes
that is the counterpart of eating.

With eating, we found a "natural" practice that is specially charged with the demand that it be a demonstration that we are *not* natural, but, rather, cultured, mannered. This significance is perhaps even more profoundly present in our engagement with reality through urinating and defecating. Like sleep, these excretory practices are practices that are largely "involuntary" in that the bodily necessity for these practices is a compulsion we experience as thrust upon us. Nonetheless, like sleep, we learn as children that we have some capacity to control how we engage in these practices, and "toilet training," as Freud's psychoanalysis stresses, is a large and very significant part of childhood education in the formation of our most basic sense of ourselves, especially our most basic sense of such notions as "will" and "propriety."

Consider what we expect of a group of adults. At a business meeting, in a classroom, or at a theatrical performance, we expect the people present to give no sign of their excretory needs or practices. An intermission will be scheduled, during which most of the participants will line up to wait for the toilets. Some, embarrassed, will have planned poorly, and will have to exit the room before or after the scheduled break in order to urinate or defecate. We expect orderly behavior from people in which their toilet habits are controlled and run on a clock that follows the schedule of the workday—surely not the situation of the young child. An inability to live by this schedule is experienced as awkward and embarrassing, both by the uncontrolled individual and by that person's companions.

Our toilet practices themselves (in the United States at least) are concealed. We lock ourselves away in "private"—that is, in exclusive, singular—rooms, where we cannot be seen or heard. We "wash our hands" of the whole affair as quickly as we can and return to a social world having effaced any evidence of this activity. We have terrible fears of these practices and demand heavy sanitation of all public-toilet areas, often demonstrating pathological—neurotic—fears about touching even the carefully scrubbed ceramic or metal fixtures with our fingers (let alone with our genitals or mouths).

"Public" toilets—that is, public "private" areas—are tense locations, for they put this activity that is supposed to be excluded from our life with others into explicit relationship with others. We can be heard, seen, and smelled by others in public washrooms. These can be tremendous sites of tension. People who are spoken to by others while in a public toilet may be unable to bring themselves to urinate or defecate, feeling so strongly the incompatibility of these actions and the company of others. People can be excited, too, about using such "taboo" sites as locations for sex, precisely for the sense of transgression and adventure they offer.

In the United States, public toilets have an interesting role to play in the structuring of masculine and feminine gender roles. Whereas women's washrooms almost without exception offer single, enclosed, private stalls for women to use, men's washrooms almost invariably have nonsecluded single urinals into which men are expected to urinate in the public company of other men. Thus, from an early age, men are forced to put their "private" things on display, and withstand the gaze of indifferent or critical others on their vulnerable private practices. Men are thus taught early to be "stoic," and to become indifferent to their bodily vulnerabilities. They must toughen themselves to the gaze of others and not admit their vulnerabilities or desires for privacy or protection of intimacy. Clearly, these themes that are raised by the simple architecture of public toilets are the central themes behind the sexist gender roles so well recognized (and criticized) in our contemporary culture. Indeed, this stoic invulnerability so definitive of masculinity is obviously the heart of the ideal of "normalcy" that we have been criticizing throughout this chapter.

We can easily see, then, how issues of personality can have their roots in our initiation and habituation into excretory practices. The issues raised by these practices—control, vulnerability, privacy, and publicity—are the building blocks of our identities, so we can also easily imagine that problems in our identities would show themselves in neurotic excretory compulsions.

Because we stigmatize urinating and defecating as dirty, we can also think of these as actions by which we cleanse ourselves, since through them we get rid of the offending dirt. The desire to purify oneself—admit to a lie or confess to a dishonest act—may show itself in a compulsive urge to urinate, to "get it out." Or, like eating, the pleasurable feelings associated with defecating—the tension and relief of the passage of the stool, the sense of wonderment at one's own accomplishment in the product (the stool)—can be the basis for a compulsion to seek out defecation, like masturbation, as a fulfilling activity to be pursued for its own sake in situations of stress.

We can be proud of our excrement. We can be impressed by the strength of our steam of urine and turn to urinating for a sense of self-importance. Simone Beauvoir, indeed, notes the significant difference in the experience of boys who can stand and "shoot" their urine in a gesture of power and self-control from that of girls who must squat and make themselves vulnerable in order to urinate. And of course, because of the intense investment our society encourages us to put into the size and power of a man's penis as a mark of sexual and therefore personal worth, it is easy to imagine the overlap of these issues onto the penis in its excretory role. Also, because humans can learn of the causal relation between eating and defecating, the issues attached to eating can be carried into the sphere of defecating. Defecating, like vomiting, can be a gesture of refusal, a show of self-improvement in "controlling one's weight/appearance," and so on.

All of these issues, of course, take us back to the scene of early family life, in which we are initiated into these practices and their attendent issues. Once again, it is the way our familiar others lead us into interpersonal life through these primitive bodily practices that shapes for us the way we will live in our interhuman bodies and places, how we will become familiar with these themes through our bodily contacts, our sketches. Urinating and defecating, like walking, sleeping, and eating, are among the most important bodily bases for our developed human identities.

As contacts with the intersubjective, these primitive bodily comportments open onto some of the most fundamental powers that we will rely upon throughout our whole history of self-transcending: these are the very "figurings" of "openness" as such. It is the basic ability—and need—to rely securely upon an intersubjective base (like the earth we walk on), and the ability to retain—return to—our selfsame identity through change that is revealed to us through sleep. Our basic capacity to take care of ourselves is revealed in eating. Finding that these compulsions are "underdetermined," that is, finding that one can have some shaping control of circumstances within the domains of these compulsions ("freedom") is originally figured in excreting. In walking we enact primitively our ability actively to take on and move forward in projects that lead us outside our present actuality. These are among the powers that make possible our more developed activities of self-transcending personhood, and it is these early childhood experiences that initiate and permanently figure these capacities as we will be able to deploy them in later life.

Our openings onto human significance are bodily, and it is thus as bodies that we initially contact other persons. Sexuality is the sphere in which this particular significance of our own embodiment is revealed to us *as such*. Sexual experience is the experience of our embodiment as the locus of *intersubjective* contact and compulsion. In erotic experience, we experience the presence of others *in our bodies*, that is, we experience the nonisolability of our bodily identity from the significance others place upon it: we experience ourselves as *essentially* living in the perspectives of other persons.

In later life we find others within our bodies when we lose our voices in front of an audience or when we experience genital changes in the presence of others who excite our interest. As humans we also have a "natural" system specially prepared for this sexual significance, and this is the genital-reproductive system that is engaged in puberty, but all bodily practices can become routes for sexual experience. By the time of puberty, this new sexual sphere has already been substantially prefigured through the bodily appropriation of intersubjectivity enacted by the child. This sexual experience is manifest primarily in the experience of bodily pleasure that the child feels in the promise of the parents' presence or the pain of longing in the parents' absence. The desire for the other is not, for the child, initially a "theoretical" stance, but for an immediate bodily sense of pleasure and pain—a mood shaping its entire environment. The distinctively sexual sphere is the sphere in which the child—and later, the adult—engages with these pleasures and pains through (more and more developed) bodily practices. Suckling at the breast is tasty, to be sure, and as such it is a response to the bodily pleasures of taste, but it is equally a way of enacting the pleasure of the company of the mother, and to the extent that that is what is contacted through suckling, the child is being initiated into sexual life.

What are these sexual feelings, these feelings of pleasure and pain that attach to being in the perspective of another—that are, indeed, the bodily experience of another's perspective? Shame and pride are probably the most familiar feelings of this sort. The glow of pride is the feeling of the other's approbation coursing through one's body, just as shame is the feeling of the other's critique pulsing within one's flesh. Love, respect, lust, and so on are variants within this arena of the bodily appropriation of the other's assessment of oneself. Sex is the originary bodily contacting of those themes of domination and cooperation that we considered in chapter 4.

Distinctively sexual neuroses will attach to the body experienced as thus "for others." Clearly, the important role of social judgment in all of our former discussions of neurotic situations indicates that in an important sense this sexual dimension is at play in all the neurotic phenomena. Nonetheless, there are compulsions that more obviously target the sexual body as such.

The erotic sphere is, of course, notorious for the place within it of the experience of compulsion. Sexual desire is itself felt as a compulsion—an uncontrollable urge—and within sexual life people characteristically have overpowering specific desires, often of a sort they are reluctant to admit. People feel driven by the urge to be urinated on, to watch their partners masturbate, to dress in clothes that typically attach to the other sex, to be spanked, tied, insulted, and so on. Sexuality is also a sphere of great distress, often attached, as are the neuroses in other bodily spheres, to the complex ambiguity of activity and passivity in sexual behaviour. "Premature ejaculation," "frigidity," and "impotence" are all familiar as forms of distress that address this facet of our sexual life. They, like sleep, are gestures that function outside the realm of immediate choice, such that we experience these bodily problems as out of our own control, even as they are clearly indications of contingent personal attitudes and not organic conditions. Sex is the arena in which we ourselves—ourselves as bodies—are most subject to judgment and criticism inasmuch as it is *as* subject to such appraisal that we *desire* to *be*, inasmuch as we *want sexual* existence. In being sexual, we thus opt for a position of being scrutinized and appraised, and it is thus not surprising that the erotic sphere, as the site where vulnerability is the defining theme, is the site of many of the most profound distresses.

Our neurotic comportment toward our sexuality is not found primarily in "odd" or exotic behavior, however. Our neuroses are primarily manifest in what is usually deemed a "normal" sexual life. To see this, we must consider more fully the distinctive character of the sexual sphere. Let us approach this by first considering some misconstruals of the sexual sphere.

There is a common prejudice—related to the prejudices we considered in the opening chapters—that construes sexuality as "bodily" rather than "mental" or "spiritual," natural rather than cultural, self-centered and desirous rather than other-directed and moral, base rather than proper. We have already seen the untenability of these sorts of dualisms in general, and our discussion of sex as the experience of our embodiment *as* the site of intersubjective contact shows in particular why these common portrayals of sexuality misrepresent its character in a deep and essential way.

Based on our earlier studies, we could recognize that these mis-
portrayals of sexuality are based on a presumption of a mind-body dualism, they are based on a quasi-religious presumption that there exists a
"given" moral order independent of the originary realm of human significance, they are based on a failure to acknowledge the self-transcending
character of human experience, and they are based on the presumption
that the human individual exists in metaphysical isolation from others.
But if we turn to a phenomenological consideration of sexual experience
itself, we can see more exactly the misrepresentative character of these
prejudices about sexuality. Sex is not a juxtaposition of one physical
mass with another; it is not a mechanical process for producing orgasm
through genital stimulation; it is not a practice for the reproduction of
the species. All of these features are indeed at play within the sexual
sphere, but they are not definitive of it. Sex *is* the experience of one's
embodiment as a locus of intersubjectivity, and for this reason issues of
pride and shame, of power, of education, of communication, of beauty,
of truth, and of goodness are as integral to erotic life as are the dynamics
of genital experience. (As a counter to these prejudices, Plato's *Symposium* remains one of the richest explorations of the complex significance
of erotic experience.)

• It is our sexual experience that is the original epiphany of the other
person, and our sexuality is the arena of person-to-person contact: we, as
persons, are in touch with other persons. Our sexual practices are thus
gestures: they are expressions of or commentaries on our interpersonal attitude and experience. Sex is the epiphany of the other, and the substance of our sexual life is how we bear witness (or fail to) to this
epiphany. The erotic experience of another is the experience of the freedom of mutual creativity, of codefinition. In our sexual encounter, it is
"up to us" to shape what will be. Here, with this other person, we are actually enacting our identity, and we need not be constrained by established norms, by others' familiar perceptions of ourselves, and so on.
Sexuality is the sphere in which our initiative, our freedom, is decisive.

As the site where our reality is not ready-made but awaits creation,
sexuality can be experienced as deeply liberating, joyful, or playful, but
equally as intimidating, frightening, or destructive. It is here that we encounter the cocreative character that is definitive of our humanity, and
our sexual behavior will be our gesture of affirming or denying this nature.

A woman is aggressively flirtatious, apparently having as a primary
goal of her actions to communicate that she is a sexual being. She keeps

her body fit and she dresses according to the latest fashions. Alone with her sexual partner, she plays out the role of the desirable woman as this is defined through television, advertising, and so on. She moves her body, makes gestures and expressions, and touches her partner as the women in the movies do. She also likes to "playfully" interrupt these practices to heighten the tension of her partner's expectations before following these actions through to the point that the partners are fully engaged in intercourse, or until her partner has an orgasm, or until there is some other "consummation" of the sexual activity.

A man, this woman's regular sexual partner, maintains an attitude of cool confidence, both in his socializing and in his private bodily interaction with his partner. He maintains a "trim" body that he is proud to display to his partner. He welcomes his partner's "erotic" stylings as she plays out the role of "sexy woman," but he is low-key in his expression of this. When they engage in coitus, he always brings his partner to orgasm before ejaculating himself, a fact of which he is (quietly) proud. Both he and his partner are careful to be tidy about their bodily fluids, and there is always a cloth at the ready to wipe away the semen if the man should ejaculate onto his or her body.

This couple, to all appearances, is close to the paradigm of proper sexuality according to the images that circulate most broadly in contemporary culture. In fact, though, their behavior evinces a substantial neurotic refusal of sexuality.

In their sexual actions, both members of this couple are guided by the goal of reproducing alien norms and an alien image of sexuality. Far from being the defining center of creative sexual activity, the experience of the other person has become a means for enacting a project of looking a certain way, a project of displaying oneself as a success in the eyes of implied others. Each partner does not engage with the singularity of the other, but uses the encounter as an opportunity to pretend to be something to a universal audience, to others in general. Whatever mutuality there is in their experience is really to be found in their cooperative support of each other in this outwardly directed project of refusing intimacy in favor of a public image.

For this couple, sex has become a site for posturing, for conforming to the rule of an image: "this is what we're supposed to do." Such an attitude is antithetical to the inherent character of sexuality as the arena of cocreation, that is, the arena where we are beyond alien rules. The behavior of these people is built around control (of image and of orgasm), around adherence to authority (the rule of the image and of public opinion), and around the domination of the other (her "playfully" asserting her power by giving or withdrawing her touch and his always ensuring that he does not "give in" to orgasm before her). In their behavior, each partner is also tacitly working to reinforce the behavior of the other. Their behavior toward sex is a fearful defense against the responsibilities and the freedom of sex, and an attempt to conceal this defensiveness through adopting a pretense of intense sexuality. Each partner tacitly protects the other from being exposed in this pretense, and they jointly establish a virtually closed system for the evasion of sexuality. (Indeed, the closed sphere they produce between themselves mirrors in many ways the logic of family relations and familial narratives of self-interpretation.)

As the sphere of personal cocreation, sexuality is inherently a sphere of communication and mutual self-definition through self-expression. Its very nature is to be oriented around the singularity of the person of each participant (hence the problem of the imposition of an impersonal and generic image), and the exchange of sexuality is thus analogous to the form of venture and responsiveness in a conversation. And, like a conversation, the subtlety and richness of sexual life grows and develops in sophistication through its ongoing enactment. Sexuality is by its nature resistant to "normalization" and rules, because of their static, impersonal, and imposed nature, but this does not mean that sex is without norms; its norms, however, are the immanent norms that develop through the contact between the partners, the norms of human contact itself with all that they entail.

Consequently, everything in our human experience circulates through our sexuality. It is primarily as human experience that our manifold contacts are ultimately significant, and so, as the direct engagement with our humanity, our sexuality is our contact with the core of all these other significances. Thus in our sexuality our most definitive and intimate human concerns are at play—our aspirations, our fears, and so on—as well as all that is built into that human experience—our parents, to be sure, but also our eating, our walking, our homes, our possessions. All of these players that populate our world are on the horizon of our sexuality, and our erotic experience can take the route of actually drawing on any of these potential resonances. Perhaps I can only feel sexually comfortable on a mattress that lies directly on the floor, or only when my father is out of town; perhaps I can only have an orgasm if you are partially clothed; certainly we cannot fully separate our sexual feelings for each other from our feelings for our parents and for our former sexual partners. The entirety of our human experience is the material out of which our sexual contact is developed, and our cocreation will always resonate with the ways in which our identities have been formed through these manifold determinacies.

As gestural, our sexual behavior can be a flight from the cocreation of erotic contact or it can be its embrace. The embrace is an embrace of the other as a self-transcending, intersubjective, erotic body. The embrace of that other will precisely be the engagement with that other as figured, as determinate: sex is with the lived body, not the reflective image of that body, which means that it is the achievement of intimacy through the embrace of the other as a manifold of figured contacts. Thus, it is not accidental that everything in our experience circulates through our sexuality: as the pursuit of intimacy, sexuality is precisely the pursuit of the other as this manifold of contacts.

For this reason, it is clear that there are norms within sexual life, but of necessity they are the norms that only arise immanently from the specific figurings of the partners and they must not be norms imposed upon the situation. There will thus always be problems in principle with laws governing sexual behavior, because sex by its very nature must reject the rule of alien norms in favor of the immanent imperatives of personal contact.

This notion of immanent norms also explains why the sexual and the genital should not be confused: the genitals are aspects of the figuring of the self-transcending human body, and for that reason their significance is not static and given, but is dynamic, variable, and something that is developed uniquely within the experience of the person. What the meaning of the genitals is for that person cannot be determined outside the immanent norms of the single individual. For all of us, much sex happens apart from the genitals, and it can be the case for some that sexuality excludes genital interaction entirely; on the other side, the life of genital contact can be devoid of sexuality, for example, in a couple who routinely enact established patterns of genital touching within a life of mutual neglect.

The enactment of roles, the imposition of laws, or the fixing of an essence to sex in, for example, procreation or genital pleasure are all forms of flight from sexuality. If one seeks the essence of sexuality, it is perhaps best found in the notion of honesty. Sex is the sphere of self-presentation and of other-reception in its most intimate and singular form. It is fundamentally these notions of self-expression and responsiveness to the other that define this sphere, and these are the basic notions of communication. The sphere of communication—of language—is thus the offspring of our sexuality.

In sex, we connect bodily with others in an arena of judgment and criticism. Fundamentally, our language is a development of this same intersubjective trajectory. In our language we endeavor to make these intersubjective contacts more articulate and to bring their parameters more within our powers, that is, we seek to increase the extent to which we can be active in this environment. Dictionaries and language instruction courses construct an illusion that our language is a neutral instrument to be utilized to accomplish specific tasks, but our living involvement in language makes it clear that this is not so. It is through language that we first become legitimate members of a community, and developing language skills—whether our native language or a second language—is very clearly interwoven with issues of self-esteem and social legitimation (rather like the issues involved in the child's developing the ability to walk). We can be soothed by another's words, hurt to our core, erotically stimulated, and so on. These are hardly neutral, instrumental situations of information-transfer! Poetry, and "literature" in general, highlights this fundamental way in which our identities are intimately interwoven with our words. We show this affective side to our language through our development of distinctive modes of speaking and writing ("style"), through crippling neurotic inabilities to speak in public or in crisis situations, through slips of the tongue, and so on.

Such phenomena should not surprise us, for it is in this arena of communication—the arena of sex and language—that we engage with the most personally affecting issue in our human experience, namely, the struggle to negotiate our self-identity in light of the experience of others, and again we should therefore expect that we will see the troubles of family life and so on put on display in our sexual and linguistic behavior. Now because our reality is largely established through habitual patterns of action in the world and habitual patterns of interaction with others, the identity we typically express is an habitual identity, sufficiently expressed through habitual patterns of language. Language, however, has a character fundamentally different from this habitual use in our more serious and more intimate affairs, and here we cannot hide behind the comfortable veneer afforded us by well-worn clichés, well-worn patterns of expression and articulation. As we have seen, it is in these most intimate relations that we face the greatest demand to *be* free: to be responsible, autonomous, cocreative, and honest. It is in our language that we most directly face this freedom, this demand to assume one's authority in the realm of the authority of the other. In our language our intersubjective reality is actually created. We are called upon to bring our reality into articulation for another, and through this articulating to engender and form a relationship with that other. In language we face the extreme pressure of honesty; we put our powers—our intelligence, our insight, our poise, and our style—on display without any pre-given limits or rules. Language, as the development of our sexuality, is the most profound sphere of self-presentation, of self-expression. It is in our language that we both have the greatest power to shape and realize our intersubjective, free reality, and that we find our reality to be most nakedly on display. Indeed, language is the sphere in which our intersubjective reality of interpersonal recognition is most properly embodied and realized, and thus is the ultimate terrain of our neurotic experience. Thus, in addition to neurotic behaviors that target explicitly the practices of linguistic expression (loss of voice, stammering, etc.), we should, indeed, recognize that *all* neurotic behaviors are essentially forms of language—the language of anorexia, the language of insomnia—inasmuch as each is a form of expressing our most personal commitments in the sphere of intersubjective recognition. As intersubjective gestures, neurotic behaviors are most fundamentally to be *read*, to be engaged with as entries in discourse.

Because language is the development of our sexuality—it is the articulation of our being-with others—it too is structured by the overarching theme of whether it enacts a flight from the experience of the other into strategies of domination and denial or an embrace of the vulnerability of mutual creation. To understand the presence of neurosis in language, it is in light of these concerns that we must consider our communicative practices.

Speaking and writing are our taking of our intersubjective reality into ourselves and giving it voice, *saying* it, and, moreover, saying it *to* another. In language, we say ourselves to each other, and our speaking, therefore, carries the weight of our own self-image, our sense of the other and the feeling both that our capacities for bearing this weight are summoned and that their adequacy is under scrutiny. Our words do not sit neutrally in some other place, but are the very making of the distance or the nearness between us. It is precisely through our language that we become close to another or that we erect a barrier between ourselves and that other.

Speaking and writing are the most fully developed aspects of our language, but language itself is the broader phenomenon of our entire gestural bearing toward others. Speaking and writing themselves never occur in isolation, but are always situated in a larger context of gestural interaction, and the relation between our explicit utterances and the larger gestural background is crucial for understanding the meaning of these articulations. We can understand this if we first notice a typical prejudice about language.

As has just been intimated, it is a typical prejudice to see language as a neutrally descriptive overlaying that is a tool for information-transfer (hence the dualism of "literal" and "metaphoric"). As did the various prejudices we considered earlier, such a prejudice rests on a misinterpretation of the world as static and already given, and wrongly divorces determinacy from its situatedness in the dynamic project of self-transcending human contact. It is our reliance on this false prejudice that keeps us from noticing that language actually *does* something: it does not just report information *about* a situation, but actually *engenders* the figuring of the human situation. Language is not a neutral "descriptive" overlaying of an already established human reality, but is the very performance or creation of that reality.

The meaning of our expressions is found in the interplay of their describing and their performing, between what they explicitly say and what they implicitly do. Our communication, our language, can thus only be understood in terms of a logic of the interplay of figure and background, of explicit and implicit, of saying and doing, and in general it will be the disparity between or the compatibility of these two aspects of our language that will be most crucial for determining the meaning of expressions. Whereas the embrace of cocreation will largely rest in the careful attending to the consonance of these two aspects of expression, flight from cocreation in language will fundamentally be enacted in the space of this disparity between the implicit and the explicit, the doing and the saying.

We can see the way that the implicit side of language is operative in the familiar scenario of the person who says, "I am sorry," but acts in such a way—through eye movements, facial expressions, tone of voice, and general bodily comportment—as to indicate that this is no genuine apology. Here, what is communicated explicitly through the words and what is communicated implicitly through the bodily gestures are at odds, and the overall communication gives the lie to the explicit utterance.

As in sexuality, so in language the flight from cocreation can be seen in the use of language to effect a pretense. A young woman finds social interactions both desirable and intimidating. Faced with a developing conversation among her companions, she feels a need to be recognized as "part" of the conversation. Her speech—which often entertains her companions, especially those who do not know her well—is filled with "hip" words and currently stylish phrasings. The content of her stories is composed from narrations of various daily affairs described in such a manner as to highlight an unusual aspect, and also to make clear that the narrator is involved in colorful activities, and "in the know" about important matters. In fact, her speech is constant posing, a constant attempt to make herself look "involved" and "in the know" when in fact she both feels and in many respects is an outsider to the arenas her conversations focus on. This woman is not ignorant of the "doing" character of speaking; on the contrary, she is very much *using* her language in an effort to induce an effect in her listeners. But hers, note, is not the stance of one who is *engaged*, but rather of one who looks on and manipulates. She is not *engaged with* her interlocutors, but is rather trying to *do something* to them. This is a defensive flight from engagement into domination. It is not a surprise to learn that this same woman describes herself as not having sexual feelings and has been pathologically concerned with suppressing her desires to eat, for the sake of establishing a "good" (thin) appearance. She is also painstaking in her choice of clothes and home-furnishings, all chosen to be appropriately current and stylish.

This woman's actions evince a fundamental ambivalence toward being with others, on the one hand finding others to be desirable prizes whose company is to be sought, and on the other hand finding them threatening forces to be manipulated and defended against. Both sides of this ambivalence contain a problem, for whether conceived as prizes to be won or forces to be controlled her others are not being engaged realistically as persons with whom one *shares* a reality, but simply as closed, alien things. Her situation with others is fundamentally one of struggling with them as alien forces, a structure rooted in a cold and impersonal family life dominated by an authoritarian father who demanded "proper" form in behavior and appearance and complemented by a mother whose dominant strategy for interacting with others was to appease those more powerful and to deliver manifest words of praise that were in fact veiled criticisms to those less powerful. Both parents made themselves unapproachable aliens to the child, and equally never approached her for the sake of developing a shared intimacy, but instead made family dealings a matter of competing for praise. It is this familial initiation into the forms of intersubjective life that this woman continues to play out in her linguistic struggles with others.

It is clear, furthermore, that this grappling with others is the significance that dominates this woman's contact with virtually every aspect of her world: her eating, her furnishings, her clothes, and the things and actions that become materials for stories are all lived through by her as sites (potential or actual) for enacting this struggle. All of her contacts are her intersubjective contacts, offering both the resources for self-transcending cocreation, and the neurotic binds that motivate her perpetually to draw these contacts into the habitual interpretive modes of flight and domination.

On the surface, this woman's actions are friendly and happy. In fact, however, her actions are an expression of unhappiness, insecurity, and fear that has been channeled into an attempt to dominate her companions. This is the sense in which there is an inherent disparity or dishonesty within her language (despite the fact that the words of her stories are all "literally true"); this whole comportment toward language thus enacts a more elaborate version of the same basic structure we witnessed in the insincere expression of apology. We can also see this structure in neurotic compulsions in general.

Fundamentally, our neurotic compulsions are intersubjective gestures—they are ways of communicating—but this is not the form of their explicit self-presentation. Anorexia and bulimia, for example, are typically described as "eating disorders," and this is true enough, but only provided that eating is itself recognized as a sexual and communicative practice. Discussions of these neurotic conditions are often unsatisfactory precisely because eating is understood in a reductionistic sense, and the sexual or gestural core of the neurotic condition is missed entirely. And indeed it is the very nature of these conditions effectively to insist on this misconstrual: "this is about eating, not about sex" is how the anorexic behavior presents itself. Again, one finds oneself "hung up" over sleep or walking, and one does not immediately see that this is a veiled way of grappling with one's parents and with their invasive behavior. Indeed, to learn that one's compulsions are interpretable gestures is a major accomplishment and a difficult one (indeed, this is a recognition to which we often have great resistance). This means that the very nature of neurotic compulsions is to enact communicative gestures the significance of which stands at odds with their manifest self-presentation. There is a way, in other words, in which the very logic of neurotic behavior is a variant of the disparity we initially noticed in the example of the insincere apology. Because our behaviors are ultimately engaged in our project of self-definition through intersubjective confirmation, it is ultimately this logic of expression and the disparity between the implicit performance and the explicit description that we must turn to in order to understand our neurotic situations.

In all of these scenarios, we have been describing human experience in terms of its self-expressive and self-interpretive aspects. This dimension of experience is such a powerful site for neurotic tensions precisely because it is so definitive of our human reality. Indeed, it is precisely the arena wherein we define ourselves. In our expressions, we take over the very dynamism of embodiment itself and *give ourselves determinate shape*. The sphere of intersubjective life is the sphere of cocreation, which means that its nature and its parameters are not established in independence of the activity of the participants. In this sphere, therefore, our identity is not something given to us but is rather something we must create for ourselves.

In our sexuality and our language we feel the burden of this, our active nature most intensely. These facets of our existence are roughly at the opposite end of the spectrum from sleep, which, as we have seen, is fundamentally the experience of our (trusting) passivity. In our intersubjective contact, on the contrary, we experience our activity; we bear the weight of responsibility for our own existence. We experience these spheres (rightly) as the measure of our true nature, and how we bear up under this measure is precisely what, we might say, is being measured. It is in this arena that we experience the inability of escaping from our responsibility for our own selves, our freedom.

Our language, whether words or background gestures, is where we "own up" to our reality. We put ourselves on display and commit ourselves to a determinate reality: I said *exactly these* words, which are now a public possession open to scrutiny and judgment. I made *exactly this* gesture, and can now always be held answerable for having done so. In our expression, we commit ourselves, such that our future will always be answerable to this past. Our language is thus *decisive*: it is where we enact the decisions regarding who we will be, what self-expressions we will carry forward as the public evidence of who we have shown ourselves to be. In our expressive behavior we decide how our intersubjective identity will be determinately embodied, and, like all embodiment, it will be the horizons opened up by this self-transcending determinacy that will set the powers and possibilities for this identity. It is in this deciding that we explicitly admit or deny, own up to or disown, our own behavioral selves. Here we will determine which of a number of possible selves we will interpret as our "real" one. Here we will resist or accept the interpretations of ourselves presented by our companions. This contact with the responsibility for ourselves can, of course, be very intimidating. The norm in our dealings with others is to rush to cover over the freedom and creativity—and the responsibility—that opens up in this sphere.

This rushing to be free of the pressure—the vertigo—of cocreation is evident conversationally when a person resorts to clichés: an issue arises calling for engagement and the pressure of the topic is deflected by the hasty halting of the engagement through the insertion of a ready-made response. This familiar practice of day-to-day conversation can be a person's entire, habitual conversational style, such that conversation as such is constantly deflected. Another person constantly defers the moment of engagement by speaking in sentences that never end, allowing his interlocutor no opportunity to respond to what has been said; this speaker seems to recognize that he is in fact undermining the possibility for real engagement, for he will never make eye contact with the person to whom he is speaking. Another person loses entirely her ability to speak precisely when it is an issue of examining her own earlier speech, precisely when it is made explicit that exactly what she says and has said will be decisive for evaluating her. These are all patterns of language neurosis, all crippling habits of defending oneself from the pressures of intersubjective life, all compulsions called up for the person by the very nature of participation in the communicative sphere.

There is an analogous but more aggressive avoiding of the responsibilities of cocreation in various practices by which persons attempt to hide behind the nonverbal character of their behavioral expressions. It is common for people to communicate much through their behavior, but then to disown this expression, defending their denial through reliance on the fact that, "I never said that." One can find another's behavior threatening, insulting, or flirtatious and, indeed, the other's behavior can indeed be such an expression, but the other can deny in each case that he or she made such an expression. An anorexic teenager may be seething with anger at her parents, and this may be what her weight loss bespeaks, and yet she can be the very model of friendly politeness in her explicit speech to them. Indeed, the ability to disown the meaning of her behavior may be essential to her ability to deal with her parents at all, for her familial narratives may have educated her to see her parents as "those who cannot be criticized." In this case, the concealing of her angry renunciation of them in disownable behavior may be as much a concealing of this from herself as it is a concealing of this from them, since the familial narrative *she* lives by would indict *her* with wrongdoing if she were to have this attitude.

Hiding in disownable gestures can thus be a terrified flight from the responsibility of cocreation, it can be an embrace of manipulative patterns for dominating the other, or it can be a self-defensive strategy for preserving one's mental health in an oppressive context. In every case, however, it remains true that this behavior is expressive. How we behave *is* decisive in our interpersonal cocreation, and so the disowning practiced by these people is ultimately untenable as a self-interpretation. The attitude of disowning rests again on the familiar positivistic prejudices that treat the world as a fully finished realm of discrete, present objects that possess their significance in independence of human sense-making, and that accordingly treats language merely as literal description or metaphoric ornament. On the contrary, *all* the determinacies of our living reality are sites for interpersonal expression and, just as everything circulates through our sexuality, so do we express ourselves throughout the entirety of our taking up of our world—in our way of living, and not just in our explicit words.

As the example of the anorexic teenager indicates, this expressive character of our behavior can be concealed from ourselves, just as it is concealed from others. Indeed, we have seen throughout our study that we do not begin from a position of perfect self-knowledge but are, rather, opaque to ourselves. Ascertaining who we are is, in fact, the fundamental struggle we are engaged with in our human sense-making, and this struggle is very much carried out through intersubjective exchanges in which it is precisely the narratives for interpreting the deteminacies of our behavior that is at issue. For this reason, the expressive sense of our most fundamental behavior is typically not clearly understood by ourselves.

We have seen that the core of our developed behavior—our neurotic posture—is to be found in the sedimentation of modes of interpretive contact in habits. This habitual core of our personality is as much habituation to modes of self-interpretation as it is habituation to characteristic construals of others. The result of this is that our neurotic habits, themselves developed in the complex and inherently opaque realm of emergent familial negotiations, bring with them habits of interpretation developed in these same negotiations with familial narratives that gave rise to the habitual practice. To our habitual action thus belong habitual self-interpretations that are, effectively, the clichés by which we have come to conceal these practices as sites for questioning and self-transformation. Thus in our relation to our neurotic practices, we face a range of options analogous to those we saw emerging in interpersonal communication in general: the vertigo of cocreation, the diversion of cocreation into clichés, and the authentic bearing witness to our cocreative reality in erotic, originary expression. Let us turn now to this erotic speech in which we resist our habitual clichés of self-interpretation and instead appeal to our expressive performances to facilitate our self-transcendence.

This erotic expression occurs when we feel our engagements with others *as* a demand for original articulation, which means that we feel the insufficiency of our habitual modes of expression and interpretation. The most familiar phenomena of such expression are in the arts—painting, music, dance, and poetry—which are precisely marked by the constancy of the effort to redefine our media of expression and, indeed, to redefine what these media can express. We see such originary expression as well in the efforts at expressing love that are the founding gestures by which a couple creates and shapes itself, "those stumbling words that told you what my heart meant," as Holt Marvell's lyrics to the song "These Foolish Things" put it (a song, incidentally, that nicely expresses the way in which our intersubjective life is embodied in the things of our world). In the religious sphere, the transformative power of honest self-expression is similarly what is targeted in the practice of confession in the Catholic Church, and perhaps more broadly in the practice of prayer in general as this is construed in various modern religions. And such erotic expression is especially developed in the projects of therapy, education, and philosophy itself.

The project of therapy is precisely the project of engaging the erotic, expressive sphere for the sake of facilitating the self-transcendence of the neurotic determinacies of our habitual situatedness. In therapy, we use expression—we cocreate with the other—to determine what our habitual comportment already expresses, for the sake of transforming this fundamental expression. Therapy seeks empowerment through liberating our expressive capacities, creating a new identity for ourselves beyond the repetition of our clichés of habitual behavior and self-interpretation.

Therapy, in other words, is the very embrace of the erotic dimension of our life as the recognition of our neurotic posture. Since this project fundamentally involves the development of understanding of the significance of the determinations of our world, it is clearly of a piece with the project of education in general; and, since this therapeutic contact involves taking our identity and the identity of the world as a question through the critical challenge to our habitual prejudices, it is clearly of a piece with the practice of philosophy. We have seen that it is this family of projects that is the natural culmination of the self-transcending character of our characteristic neurotic posture, so we can now conclude our study with an outline of this trio of practices of erotic speech as characteristic elements of human experience.

In sum, then, what we have seen is that our identity (a) is fundamentally developed through the dynamics of intersubjective recognition, primarily as these are initiated in family life, and (b) is fundamentally a bodily identity. We should therefore expect that the core of our identity will be manifest at the core of our embodiment, and this is what we have been considering as we have examined characteristic neurotic tensions as they emerge in relationship to our most basic bodily practices—the practices that figure our living contact with the world. Our identity is bodily and intersubjective, which means that we contact the world neurotically through the self-transcending determinacies of the specific dimensions of our embodiment. Or, said the other way around, our embodiment is the memorializing of familial life through neurotic contacts. This is the essential human condition, and we can turn now to the issue of care, that is, the issue of how we can deal with ourselves and each other in a way that is responsive to the troubles and tensions that animate this neurotic posture.

Part III

The Process of Human Experience

6

Philosophy

Neurotic Self-Transcendence

We cannot escape our determinacy. As self-transcending, as open, it is indeed this determinacy that is our entry into all value. Nonetheless, this determinacy is also our limit in that it imparts its form to the whole realm in which we are in contact with reality. Our embodiment is a wonder and a tragedy. The wonder of our embodiment is its openness. It is through the body that the whole world of significance opens up to us, and the self-transcending character of the body is our freedom to redefine ourselves and our world. The tragedy of our embodiment is that it is a legacy we can never shake. This tragic dimension of our embodiment is the truth behind myths of pollution and blood guilt that we find in such classic tales as Aeschylus' *Oresteia* or Sophocles' *Oedipus the King*. Our embodiment carries with it the history of our family life as our neurotic compulsions, which are the memories of our initiation into the power struggles of intersubjective life as they are encoded into our most primitive bodily practices.

These neurotic compulsions cannot be removed. They are the very schemata for meaning, the developed forms by which we sense. But, though they cannot be removed, these schemata, like all bodily phenomena, are self-transcending. Our neuroses figure our contact, but they figure it in a way that always invites transformation and development. The "cure" for neurosis is not the removal of these figurings, but the development of the potentials implied within the contact these bodily comportments offer us. It is this development that we should understand by the term *therapy*.

Because "being neurotic" does not mark out the character of a specific set of people, but characterizes, rather, the essential human condition, we cannot think of "therapy" as a special practice that is geared only to the abnormal demands of select individuals. Rather, we must see that the traditional practices known as "psychological therapy" and the traditional practices geared toward "normal" human development must in truth be recognized as variants on the same theme. "Therapy" and "education," in other words, are in fact the same project. As we consider how this is so, we will see, ultimately, what "philosophy" is as a phenomenon of human, bodily contact, by recognizing in it the culmination of this project of therapy and education as the self-transcending of the neurotic posture. We have seen already that the family and the political order are institutions of human life called forth by the very nature of the body as self-transcending and intersubjective. The same is true for the practices of therapy, education, and philosophy, the practices of erotic discourse.

We always experience our situation—our present—as a tension: a tension between aspiration and achievement, between desire and satisfaction. At the most general level, this is just a restatement of our thesis from chapter 1, that our experience is inherently temporal. In other words, we always experience ourselves as on the way toward the future that we live as our goals, on the basis of the past that we live as our memory of—our holding onto—what we have in fact already established. The present is "on the way," which means that it is defined by its relation to those goals it has not yet fulfilled. The compulsions we experience as objects are the way these goals are felt by us *as* the essence of the present. In this general sense, then, the present is always a tension between aspiration and achievement. Education, in general, is learning how to act in such a way as to answer to this tension so as to satisfy these desires, these aspirations. We seek education because our situation poses a problem, a demand.

In identifying the neurotic character of our existence, we are identifying a complicating and a specifying of this tension. The tensions we feel are not always immediate and passing, but can be inherent to the very *form* of our contact. A neurosis is the way a tension—a frustration of desire—is structured into our very approach to things. What we normally call "therapy" is education geared to this tension—education geared toward alleviating the *structural* tension built into our *way* of being in the world. We seek therapy because we experience the form of our characteristic, habitual approach to problem-solving as itself a problem.

Education in general and therapy in particular have as their *raison d'être* a felt need for relief, that is, they make sense as, and only as, answers to problems experienced by persons. As with all other "sense," education makes sense only as figured by the mode of bodily contact lived by the person. It is only within the terms opened up by one's figured contact that one can be educated, that one can transcend oneself. (Indeed, this was precisely the thesis of chapter 2, "Embodiment.") Our emphasis on the body has been an insistence that it is only through (and as) the determinacy of our situations that we are anything, and that we participate in the openness to development and self-transcendence that is our freedom. Our freedom, in other words, is not freedom from what determines us, but is the freedom that opens up within this determinacy. Under the heading of "therapy," we study the process of coming to grips with our determinacy, of bringing the determinacies that *already* shape our existence into an explicitly interpretable form so that we can recognize the intelligibility that is governing our experience. When therapy is understood in this way, it is not hard to see that the practices we usually associate with the terms *education* and *science* are variants on this same therapeutic process.

As we have seen from the start, the very nature of the determinacy of our situation is to be that which makes demands upon us to respond to *its* agenda. In other words, we experience the determinacies of our world as carrying in themselves the principles of their own intelligibility. We must *learn* what these things are and how "we can" approach them through, so to speak, "asking" them. We must *study* the world, and *it* confirms or resists our efforts at interpretation and interaction. Science—knowledge—is successfully answering to the demands with which our objects confront us. In this sense, then, education is implicitly a carrying out of the project of comprehending our determinate selves that is originally launched in therapy. Let us now begin our study with this "education" as it is explicitly directed toward ourselves as form-giving agents, that is, let us begin with therapy. We will ultimately recognize that this practice of therapy is ultimately realized as the intersubjective practice of phenomenological philosophy.

Therapy

We have now come to see why the characteristic development of human contact sets "normal" selfhood as a goal and how neurotic behavior fails to meet that goal. We have also seen that the goal is flawed in itself and that the values projected by this goal stand at odds with the resolution of the problems recognized within normal selfhood. Normalcy, in other words, recognizes, misidentifies, and cannot improve the neuroses. We have, on the other hand, understood the neuroses and have produced the criteria by which they can be properly identified both as solutions to problems (in that they are the habitual ways we developed for coping with the demands of intersubjective life as we originally experienced it) and as problems in need of solution (in that they are methods for problem-solving that are out of step with the demands of our developed social existence). What we now have to do is to use this understanding to understand what it is to "solve" neurotic problems, that is, what sense there can be to the notions of "therapy" and "cure."

Let us reiterate how we can understand the notion of "illness" in order to establish how we must understand this notion of "cure." Because we do not understand the neuroses to be illnesses in any senses other than that they are situations of subjective distress or that they are situations characterized by discernible internal contradictions, their cure cannot be seen as an elimination of an evil presence that allows the person to return to an innocent, original state of health, nor can their cure be understood as a kind of "chemical" conjuring by which some ingredient happens to interact with another ingredient to create or precipitate some otherwise unintelligible result. "Cure" can only be understood here to mean care: to cure is to care for the animating needs and desiring of the suffering individual and to resolve the problems faced by that individual through facilitating and supporting the development of that person's mode of contact. The cure cannot be understood as bringing the person into accord with an alien standard of rightness, but must be understood as an answering to, and support of, demands that arise from within that person herself. It must be, in other words, the self-transcendence of the neurotic condition itself.

The neurotic person experiences compulsions—the need to eat, the need to fight, and so on. These are the responses that are demanded by the very identity of the object the neurotic faces, the very situation in which she lives. This is because, as we saw especially in chapter 3, the identities of objects—their objectivity—is forged out of memory, which means that they are an embodiment of an expression of the commitments that figure our intersubjective contact. To understand a neurotic behavior, then, requires that one understand how the specific identity of that object to which this behavior is a fulfilling response is constituted within the neurotic person's experience. In the case of the conflict of intentions that produces the experience of anxiety or distress, the commitments constitutive of the identity of the situation to which the neurotic behavior is a response are not consistent with other commitments on the basis of which the person approaches the situation. The same person, in other words, is pulled in two ways. It is imperative to notice, however, that it is the same person, and it is only because it is the same person that that person can experience the pain of the conflict. The conflict comes into being because each of the sets of commitments that shape the person's behavior claims to be an adequate and total interpretation of what is relevant and proper to the situation, so their claims necessarily pertain to the same terrain, but their claims are not compatible.

Notice that the two routes to contact cannot in this situation claim to be innocent or "just minding their own business," so to speak. The commitments we make to approaching situations have implications such that, for example, to adopt one approach to things necessarily puts one in conflict with certain other approaches. Even though, then, one did not ever intend to enter into polemical debate about which other approaches are wrong, one cannot avoid doing so, simply because of the determinate, that is, exclusive, nature of commitments. The interpretive strategies and commitments we embrace in our efforts to contact and comprehend our world are thus committed to interpretive or "epistemological" debates whether they like it or not. Each form of contact we engage in endorses and advocates a thesis, and this thesis automatically is embedded in polemical relations with other (possible and actual) theses and thus requires defense. Neurotic conflict, then, can be seen to be at root a kind of lived argument, a living struggle between two opposed claims about what the proper way is to know the truth about things. This should not be surprising, because we have known all along that the commitments are themselves strategies of understanding and interpretation that can be evaluated in terms of their adequacy. What we can see now is that the resolution of neurotic conflict is essentially a matter of "epistemological" investigation, not in the sense that therapy is necessarily "cognitive," but in the sense that conflicts are essentially conflicting theses about the nature of reality. Neurosis is an intrinsically contradictory lived interpretive stance, and the distress marks the conflict of interpretations: the distress reveals the polemical and argumentative nature of the lived theses. The resolution to this distress will amount to a testing— really, a self-testing—of these commitments as truth-claims: caring for— "curing"—this situation will ultimately amount to bringing to explicitude the interpretive commitments that are manifest as the neurotic behavior, discerning their implications, working to establish the soundness or unsoundness of these interpretive values, and engaging in practices to

develop an habituation to an alternative (defensible and desirable) interpretive stance.

Remember that the project behind our developing habits of contact
is that of becoming someone, of establishing for ourselves a particular
identity that is recognized within our intersubjective environment. The
various specific narratives and strategies that we develop have as their
premise that they are supportive of this goal. This we saw earlier when
we considered these habits as accomplishments and as defenses of identity. But this means that acting according to these habits is ultimately an
assertion that such practices are supportive of such a goal. In other
words, the commitment that is embodied in our objects and to which we
respond in such practices is ultimately this commitment to establishing
an identity within a context of intersubjective recognition. Such practices can, then, be tested to see if they do in fact support this goal.

A young woman entrusts a friend to make plans. The young woman
wants the plans to work out rightly. In her family, however, to entrust
something to another was to face mistreatment. Her parents regularly
forgot or violated promises they made to their children, and the woman's
siblings learned early the advantages that could be gained by similar
practices of winning and then violating the other's trust and vulnerability. Consequently, the young woman learned the importance of a policy
of vigilant and aggressive "checking up" on other family members who
made commitments to her. This habit of interpersonal navigation continues to shape her social life, and finding herself in a situation where she
wants good plans to be made but that another has control of them, she
responds to this object the way it has always called out to her throughout
her family life: such a situation says, "check up on that person to make
sure that person is not mishandling this responsibility." The young
woman calls her friend and demands to know the state of the plan-
making. In doing so, she annoys her friend and interrupts the friend's
work. The result is that the friend has to work late, and cannot make
plans in the way that was initially intended. The net result of the young
woman's action is that she undermined the possibility of the plans being
carried out rightly. This despite the fact that her goal was the exact opposite. In the context of an unjust family life in which family members could
not be trusted to stick to their commitments, her way of responding to the
situation by checking up on her friend was supportive of the goals she
wanted. That same course of action now has the opposite significance.
Such an action is called out of her by the situation, and initially she

cannot see how it can be anything other than the appropriate, that is, the obvious and necessary thing to do. In fact it is precisely the wrong thing to do. What explicitly comes to her in the situation is that "I must intervene," and the commitment that justifies it is left implied "in order for the plans to be carried out." In fact this claim is false—intervention is not necessary for the plans to be carried out—and this can be made explicit through reflection because the woman can agree that what she really desires is for the plan to be carried out, she can agree that this really is why it seemed to her that she had to intervene, and she can agree that her actions were in fact counterproductive. Having become habituated to such a practice of intervention means that the necessity to so act strikes her immediately. The error of this practice can be discerned only discursively. But though it is not recognized immediately, the error is nonetheless discovered on the basis of the principles that animate the immediate feeling.

A young man believes that he has evidence that he is worth nothing, having consistently had this implied to him as a child by his parents' deeds of overruling his statements of his desires and preferences, of ignoring the boundaries of his privacy, and in general of paying him little heed. On the other hand, just by being a living center of meaning he cannot deny the sense that he is someone. Throughout his day-to-day affairs he constantly contends with the immediate sense that he must be wrong to feel like he is someone. He is convinced that various events are tests of his value that will confirm this self-interpretation: in facing certain situations he immediately recognizes them as situations in which he will fail and in which he will therefore find proof of his valuelessness. When asked whether success in these events will count as evidence for his value, for his being someone, he concedes that they will not. He thereby comes to recognize that the project of interpreting these events as tests is not mounted on real principles of evidence and evaluation, though they claim to be; these are, rather, projects of interpreting in which the implied, forgotten premise is that "I am nothing" (the premise that was required for the successful navigation of family life). These situations explicitly claim to be proofs, but only based on an implied commitment to already endorsing the supposed conclusion. By claiming to be a proof, this stance makes itself open to the demand that it live up to the requirements of proof, and this supposed proof is fallacious—a circular argument; it reveals itself to be unsatisfactory according to its own principles. Rendering this fallacy explicit is crucial to stripping the supposed

proof of its unquestioned hold, for though it remains immediately, per-
ceptually gripping, it is discursively recognized as fallacious. (Indeed, the
standard informal fallacies found in logic textbooks in fact correspond in
interesting and important ways to many of the typical structures of neurotic interpretation.)

These scenarios are two examples of situations in which the mediation implicit in certain neurotic compulsions is rendered explicit in terms
of the interpretive project in which each is fundamentally engaged.
These examples focus only on isolated aspects of the total personal and
therapeutic situations of the persons involved, but they nonetheless
highlight the crucial structure in unlocking neurotic problems. When
the hidden commitments that guide our interpretive behavior are formulated as explicit argumentative theses, they are open to evaluation and
criticism by their own criteria. For the neurotic individual, bringing the
neurotic behavior to this level of explicit understanding is crucial to the
process of changing this behavior. This practice—the practice of getting
to "know oneself"—is ultimately the conceptual core to the therapy for
the neurotic individual, that human person whom each of us cannot
avoid being if we in fact grow up to the level of free functioning adults.
Our lives manifest the distresses that come from neurotic conflicts, and it
is by way of this "immanent critique"—self-transcendence by way of self-
interpretation and self-explication—that these self-contradictory aspects
of ourselves can develop to a healthier state. Therapeutic self-development
is this process of thoughtful self-explication.

The process of thinkingly explicating one's habitual moods, however, cannot simply be done immediately, for it requires practice, prepa-
ration, and a whole host of supporting changes of behavior and situation.
Furthermore, a conceptual analysis of the sort just alluded to will not immediately or by itself change one's compulsive patterns of behavior.
Therapy, that is to say, is not simply a matter of cognitive analysis but is
a rich and varied field of human experience that both draws on and relies
upon every aspect of human behavior and experience. The process of
"thinking through" has to be both prepared for and followed by other
supporting behavior and settings, has to be practiced, and has to be repeated until it has itself become a habitual and familiar mode of behavior.
This is because, as we have seen, the self who does the explicit thinking is
not immediately and precisely identical with the self who compulsively
contacts a habitual world, and the project is to *make* the thinking self—that
is, the free self who recognizes and rejects the contradictory interpretive

strategies—into the habitual self. One cannot, therefore, simply think one's way out of the problem along the model of the stoic who by an act of stern self-denial says, "I will no longer do that." Rather, one can work to make one's habitual self a thinking self by trying repeatedly to establish familiar and comfortable routes of approach to the situations that call up the compulsive behavior that are different from the old routes that one wishes to change. Therapy will ultimately be a project of rehabituation, governed by the principle of this explicit self-critique. Such a project of rehabituation will be difficult and it will be carried out over a long period of time, just as the initial project of forming the habits that constitute one's personality was carried out only over years and only as the absolutely central concern of all of one's actions. In other words, taking on the project of therapy has a scope comparable to the project of growing up, or to the project of raising a child.

To be able to explicate the commitments implicit in one's situation requires considerable practice and insight, as does any other form of analysis. (Part of the goal of this book is to facilitate people in their attempts to do just this.) Indeed, it is already a substantial change from the normal course of everyday life just to turn one's gaze away from one's usual projects and toward oneself as an interpretive, situated, bodily subject. Even having made these changes—turning one's attention and going further and developing the basic ability to discern the commitments in one's behavior—one will not thereby have "solved" one's problems. One's problems are rooted in the conflict inherent to the most deeply seated habits of making sense that found one's personality. These habits operate at a level, as it were, behind our self-conscious reflection. Thus, we can self-consciously learn truths about ourselves—about the conflicts in our habits—without thereby being able (immediately) to change those habits of interpretation. To change will require a much larger project than merely a cognitive one.

We find ourselves behaving in destructive ways that we cannot control: we find ourselves driven. At a fundamental level, our desire is to change these ways of behaving. Therapy aimed simply at reflective cognition would completely bypass the center of the problem, for, without a change in behavior, the problem persists. Therapy will thus typically also mean efforts specifically directed at action. And because the behavioral patterns that trouble us are habitual and not merely occasional, the relevant behavioral changes will also have to be at the level of habit. Thus therapy will fundamentally involve behavioral change directed toward building new habits.

One can have the good fortune simply to happen upon a set of practices that will lead to a satisfactory change in behavior, that is, people do at times improve their lives to a degree that is satisfying to themselves by following methods that have not been developed through thoughtful analysis. Realistically, however, one must expect that projects of changing one's habitual patterns in ways that will solve one's problems will require intelligence, understanding, and education in their design and then diligence and perseverance in their implementation. Our habitual behaviors *are intelligent*: they exist for discernible reasons rooted in the history of our development. Interacting with them effectively will come from understanding them, whereas attempts at behavioral change that lack this insight typically either will fail to change anything or, if there is a change, will result in the reproduction of the problem by means of a new behavioral outlet. Modifying Immanuel Kant, we can say that cognitive therapy divorced from behavioral change is largely empty, while behavioral change divorced from cognitive insight is largely blind.

To understand one's behavior, one will have, first, to understand it as expressive and especially as expressive in an intersubjective setting and expressive of one's contact with intersubjectivity. This means that it is primarily to one's relations with other persons—current and familial— that one need turn to understand one's neurotic troubles. It is in this arena that therapeutic change will ultimately have to be developed.

Second, how one contacts others will be embodied in the objects of one's world. Thus it will be through the careful description of how one experiences objects that the nature of one's intersubjective world will be "unearthed," so to speak. This understanding of how one experiences objects can also be crucial for therapeutic change, for by reconfiguring one's objective environment one can often remove the triggers of the neurotic behaviors, as well as giving one something like a "blank slate" in which to develop a new way of being in the world. Because our temporality is embodied as our objects, our places (like our families) are the originary settings that offer or withhold various modes of behavior, and so reshaping our objective setting—re-placing ourselves, as it were—is fundamental to empowering ourselves in our projects of self-transformation.

Of course, other persons will be among the most crucial members of this environment, and so how one populates one's world—with new and old friends, family members, partners and, importantly, another person who acts as a therapist—will be decisive for how effective this reembodying of one's situation will be. If one imports into one's new setting the same people—the same relationships—that either cause or trigger one's problems, one should expect little change. Eliminating the weekly telephone conversations with one's mother or terminating one's weekly visits to one's domineering and interfering friend may be what is decisive for allowing one the opportunity to "re-tool," as it were.

It is with these issues of redesigning one's setting (human and otherwise) that intelligence and the understanding of one's own behavior proves most critical. When one *understands* one's behavior, one can realistically assess and address its causes; without this understanding, one can superficially address what is perhaps a symptom, but the real source of the problem will continue doing its work, and one's attempted solution will be ineffective. Indeed, many people's rejection of therapy as unsuccessful in fact reflects only the ignorant way in which their therapeutic project was designed; the failure of poorly designed therapeutic plans is simply further testament to the need to base such practices on a sound understanding of the expressive character of one's behavior.

This task of discerning what are the problems in one's existing setting is also the area in which people enact the greatest resistance to the therapeutic project. Therapy is a process of radical self-change and self-critique, and that means change and critique of one's situation. It will typically require that one recognize terrible failings in one's parents and in one's long-established practices of acting in the world. The very habitual contact one has developed, however, will undoubtedly be built around the need not to criticize one's parents and, similarly, one will be habitually committed to the sense of the worthiness and reliability of one's long-established practices. In other words, one will typically be deeply committed to refusing to challenge the very things that therapy requires be criticized and changed. Therapy is thus a site of great conflict, both for the individual within herself and, typically, between the individual and her important others. This is as it should be, of course, because it is fundamentally the struggle of responsible understanding with the founding values of our habitual life, each a tremendously important aspect of our existence, each importantly dependent upon the other, and each attached to a radically different vision of how our lives will be carried out. It is the turning of the powers made available to us through our embodiment against the very form that that embodiment has taken. It is in this sense that therapy is immanent critique or self-transcendence: we ourselves overcome ourselves by using the very powers made available through our situation to transform that situation. The powers of intelligence and insight are our strongest resources here for they can understand the contradictions plaguing our behavior and understand what must be changed; they can be effective only in a setting that allows them room to take root and develop.

• In sum, this therapy or "thinking through" is a complex behavioral transformation, guided by the desire to understand ourselves through developing insight into the determinacies of our situation. It is engaging in creative dialogue with oneself, working to discern what is expressed through one's behavior, and developing a response that will allow one to express oneself differently. It involves a "turn" (a "conversion," as it were) of one's attitude away from the world interpreted as "objective" (i.e., the world interpreted in terms of the positivistic prejudices we have analyzed throughout) and toward oneself as the sense-giving power operative throughout one's situation. It involves educating oneself into how to describe what is expressed in one's behavior and one's settings. It involves the practice of this turning and description, repeated over time until it becomes habitual. It involves a reconfiguring of one's environment that is rooted in a project of self-critical self-understanding, and thus requires a willingness to challenge the values one habitually sees in particular persons, things, and practices. Therapy in sum is a radical self-transformation or, more exactly, the enactment of the self-transcendence of one's neurotic posture.

Notice that the one who takes on this project of therapy is necessarily the neurotic individual herself. The neurotic individual must relate to (contact) herself as one who has to grow up again, as one who has to be approached and remolded. The neurotic individual, in other words, must recognize that the "she" who is doing the practicing (of new patterns of thinking) is not immediately identical with the "she" who is to change—whom she wants to change. The individual engaged in therapy must thus approach herself as another, as an independent force and reality to be studied and approached on its own terms. Therapy thus requires that the neurotic individual recognize the inadequacy of the vision of normal selfhood. This means that part of the conceptual reorientation necessary to the thinking explication of herself will be engaging in a study of selfhood analogous to that performed in this book. Indeed, successful therapy will ultimately require that the neurotic self become something of a phenomenologist.

Therapy will thus to a large extent involve learning to describe the way in which one experiences objects, the way in which one finds situations calling upon one, how one's compulsions are experienced. This description is the first step toward the explication of these situated experiences in terms of the interpretive commitments they enact and embody, and the subsequent reeducation of one's most familiar interpretive reflexes. Therapy thus amounts, not to an escape, nor to a return to some original purity, nor to an advance to some preestablished goal of perfection, but to a phenomenological process of self-interpretation and self-transcendence. We have so far been discussing this in terms of the therapeutic subject herself. What, though, is the role of others in the process?

We have already seen that the nature of human contact is always intersubjective. This means first that we are always in search of confirmation of our sense of ourselves and of our world. It also means, second, that the projects upon which we embark are limited in their ability to come to fruition by the level of support provided by our societies, which means all of our family, our immediate circle of companions, our larger legal and political system, our traditions, and so on. Indeed, typically our neurotic problems are a result of the inadequacies of social support that we have received in our familiar, familial environments, and our ability to engage in an attempt to therapeutically transform ourselves itself emerges through our advance out of the familial environment into a larger society that advocates the values of universal humanity; and this larger level of society, too, brings trouble even as it offers liberation through its problematic ideal of normalcy. It also means, third, that one's therapeutic advance, though a development of oneself, is itself an intersubjective activity, dependent upon the support of others.

The forms of human development are open to study and investigation as much as are the forms of chemical reaction or the forms of plant reproduction, and comparable issues of ignorance and expertise are similarly raised in all of these cases. Consequently it is not at all surprising that there are people who are specially knowledgeable about neurotic conditions and their treatment. Given the picture of human life we have here sketched out, it is not at all surprising that successful therapy typically involves turning to another for guidance in what is really a project of self-transcendence. This is a natural and obvious form for realizing the structure of therapy, which, we have shown, is itself an essential element of human experience. This other person, the therapist, offers a particularly significant example of how our development requires intersubjective support. The relation of an individual to a therapist, like the relation of a family member to a family, or the relation of a citizen to a state, can

take on a variety of forms that range from specially stifling and destructive to specially liberating and constructive, and we must be careful not
to confuse therapy as an essential dimension within human meaning
with its professionalized stand-in, that is, we must judge professional
therapists by the norms inherent to the notion of therapy rather than allowing therapy to be defined by whatever "therapists" happen to practice. To be able to determine therapy's better and worse realizations
requires first a clear understanding of the role of the therapeutic relationship within the larger human drama.

Before anything else, the relation of "patient" and therapist is a relation between persons. The reason the individual looks for the therapist
probably does not primarily involve a desire to become involved in a personal relationship with that particular person who is the therapist, but
establishing such a relationship is nonetheless the inescapable condition
for engaging in the therapeutic process. These two individuals, patient
and therapist, will each be individuals approaching the other from
within their respective forms of intersubjective contact; neither, in other
words, is simply a role or an instance of a type. Furthermore, the experience of therapeutic self-transformation that is desired is profoundly intimate. Consequently this relationship, if successful, will be a particularly
significant personal interaction for each participant. Whether or not this
aspect of the relationship is given sufficient attention within the therapeutic process plays a significant role in determining the quality of
the therapy. (This inherently personal—that is, intimate, singular and
self-defining—character to the relationship is the reason for therapy's inherent resistance to professionalization, and also why it will always rest
uncomfortably with attempts to make it answerable to the impersonal
demands of legality.)

As an interpersonal relationship, this dyad must be considered in
terms of the projects with which both members enter just as the intrafamilial and various other relationships were considered in these terms
when the subject of others was initially broached in chapter 4. We need
to ask, "What does the patient desire in seeking a therapist?" and "What
does the therapist desire in seeking a patient?" The answers to these
questions will determine the basic parameters of the interpersonal dynamics that can develop within the therapeutic situation.

Therapy has been described in this chapter as an issue of education; it
is also a situation of something like the "rebirth" of the individual. Consequently we should expect the model of patient-therapist to be analogous

to the model of learner-teacher, and also to that of the child-parent. If we think, first, about the goals of education we can in fact begin to see these roles of patient and therapist more clearly. One enters into a learning relationship with a teacher because and to the extent that that teacher can speak as a representative of reality and one is oneself struggling to establish the nature of reality. One enters into a relationship with a student because and to the extent that that student is trying to establish for herself the nature of reality and one desires (or, indeed, feels compelled) to represent it. It is only when such roles are filled that the educational goals can be fulfilled. The same must be true of the therapeutic relationship.

The distinctively therapeutic relationship, however, is the relationship of education focused on the central question of one's own reality and identity as a person, that is, it is focused on the question, "Who am I?" For that reason, in picking a therapist, an individual is picking another individual to act as a representative of what it is to be human, that is, a representative of the demands of the reality of others as such. As we have seen, it is others who hold the power of confirmation or rejection of our sense of how things are, and it is this power that is put into the therapist's hands. In this respect, the therapist's educational role is a taking over of the original role of the family (and especially the parents), for we have already seen that the family is defined by its role of initiating one into the world of intersubjectivity. Thus, for the relationship between two individuals to be therapeutic, one individual must be approaching the other-as-therapist with a desire to be educated in the context of the fundamental question, "Can you tell me that I am right about me?" or something similar, while the other individual must correspondingly recognize that this is the scope of the undertaking and embrace the responsibility for caring for the unique demands of the perspective of the other-as-patient. Note that this entails, among other things, that the would-be therapist herself must *learn* from the other how that other experiences the significance of the world, since therapy must be immanent, that is, must develop from within the needs of the "patient": it cannot be a situation of imposing an already established "solution" or even "method" upon the patient understood as an example of a type. (Hence the misleading character of the term *patient*.)

In being entrusted with the confirming power of others in relationship to the fundamental question of another's identity, the therapist is thus entrusted with the individual's own most intimate needs and powers, for the therapist is made the agent who works on behalf of the individual's own identity. The therapist is thus being handed the power to speak and act on behalf of the patient's needs by speaking as a representative of others as such and as a representative of the patient's needs in relation to others. The therapist is thus charged with taking over the demands and the dynamics of the whole foundation of the individual's intersubjective contact, which amounts to the individual's entire contact with reality, her contact as such. The therapist, in other words, is entrusted with the very identity of the individual. The therapist thus becomes, in the sense of the ancient Greek religious term *therapon*, a "substitute" for the patient.

But this therapy is an intersubjective *relation*, that is, it is a dyad that is characterized by the projects of both patient and therapist. What are the desires of the therapist that define this situation? Simply by virtue of being a person, the therapist necessarily approaches the patient from within that therapist's own neurotic forms of contact. Consequently, therapy cannot simply be understood as a "one-way" affair, but must ultimately be the negotiating of the dyad shaped by the interaction of the neurotic postures of both therapist and patient. This, however, still does not yet tell us the nature of the definitive desires of the therapist as such. Precisely in accepting "patients," what is the therapist after? What is the nature of the desire that makes one a therapist properly so-called? The therapist, qua therapist, must desire to carry out the responsibilities of acting on behalf of the individual as a response to the experience of the demands of others as such. We have seen that intersubjective projects are rooted in the pursuit of self-confirmation from others. We must then ask how this project of "being the other for another" is a project of self-confirmation on the part of the therapist.

What the therapist qua therapist is after from the "patient" is recognition of the demands of objectivity as such to which the therapist finds herself to be subject, that is, the therapist is after confirmation that her contact is "objective," which means recognizable by all others as their own truth. For an individual to recognize (rightly) the necessity of the perceived demands of reality is thus equally for that individual to see the need for others to recognize their necessity, which means that the very recognition of these truths compels that individual to lead others to this recognition. In dealing with particular patients the therapist is after vindication in thinking that she was right to say that she already knew in principle what the patient wanted, that is, the therapist believes herself to know *what a person* qua *person aspires to be*, and such a truth demands universal vindication if it is in fact the universal truth it purports to be. The therapist's claim, in other words, is that she was acting as the patient's substitute—already acting on behalf of the patient's well-being—all along. So the therapist, in asking, "Am I right about you?" is ultimately asking the patient the same question the patient asks the therapist, namely, "Can you tell me that I am right about me?" Just as the therapist holds the key to the patient's identity, the patient is likewise already implicated in the therapist's identity. The therapist's truth *must* be recognizable by all when it is presented to them, so the nature of this truth is that it must be permanently put to the test.

I have just articulated the therapist's project in terms of objectivity, but to see the real significance of this it is helpful to translate this back into the terms of our initial study of recognition and confirmation. We saw in chapter 4 that seeking recognition in the eyes of others is the key to understanding our freedom, and our essentially human character, and this character as much explains the role of "therapist" as it does the role of "patient." In each case, the real issue is ultimately the search for a kindred spirit, an attempt to connect around a shared sense of the world of our experience. Therapy, or pedagogy in general, is simply the self-conscious taking up of this project of recognition, such that one pursues being–recognized through facilitating the recognizing of others. The therapist wants to offer the other individual the claim that "I recognize you," and wants this effort itself to be recognized for what it is—the therapist, thus, really asks, "Are you a kindred spirit?" or, equally, "Am I right to say that I recognize you?"

This more impersonal talk of objectivity and the more personal talk of "kindred spirits" can both be translated into the standard terms of ethics. To say that the therapist is self-conscious about the essentiality of the dynamics of intersubjective recognition is to say that the therapist recognizes that our self-transcending experience fundamentally propels us beyond ourselves to the realm in which we recognize that *for ourselves* the other's perspective is an essential value, and something for which we must care. Our essential reality as persons *is* to be drawn out of ourselves by others, and only thereby to arrive at ourselves. Therapy is the culmination of this experience of other selves for it is the stance in which we recognize that the care of ourselves is the care for others. For this reason, it is clear that "therapist" does not specially name the members of an established profession, but names rather a human role whose values pertain to all of us in our dealings with our fellows.

Of course, actual relations of therapy need not live up to this logic. Persons certainly can—and perhaps typically do—put themselves into professional positions of therapy in order to act out their own neurotic compulsions toward dominating others, persons with sound intentions can be ignorant of what the demands of therapy require and can misinterpret and mislead the individuals who come to them for help, and, of course, individuals can seek therapy on the basis of a wide range of motivations that undermine the successful carrying out of the therapeutic relationship. What we have, seen, though, is the rationality behind such therapeutic relations, and therefore, the immanent norms of this practice that should guide our interpretation of the practices in which we actually do engage.

This understanding of therapy can again allow us to see why it is inherent to therapeutic practices to operate within a sphere characterized by conflict and resistance. The intimate bond of mutual trust upon which the relationship of therapy is premised is not just a conceptual challenge to the ideas that governed one's family life, but is the establishment of a new "home," as it were. The bond with the therapist must become the site of truth for the "patient," though this is originally the significance that the family claims for itself. The therapeutic relationship by its nature calls for a radical decision—a living, behavioral decision, not simply an intellectual decision—to establish a new home in a new human experience that is inherently in conflict with the established experience of family life. Therapy is only realized in a transformation within one's intersubjective relationships, and thus invites upon itself animosity and opposition both from the patient's significant others and from the patient's own habitual protectiveness of its relationship to those others. It is for this reason especially that an understanding of the inherently personal nature of the therapeutic situation is crucial to its successful development.

Here, then, we have the basic logic of the essential human relationship of therapy. This relationship is essentially a development at a self-conscious level of the original relationship that constitutes the family, in that it is the attempt to pursue rigorously and by choice the entry into the demands of intersubjectivity by way of another individual—inasmuch, that is, as therapy reenacts the intersubjective determining of an individual's identity by means of another's assuming the role as representative of others as such. It is also a transcendence of the "givenness" of family life to the extent that the participant in the figure of the parent—that is, the therapist—explicitly recognizes the reciprocity of the structure of recognition that is at play here, that is, the therapist qua therapist is seeking from the "patient" a recognition that is ultimately the same in form as that which the "patient" seeks from the therapist.

As well as being a transformative development of the relations that constitute familial life, the therapeutic relationship also anticipates the educational relationship in general. This is not hard to see, if we recall the project of therapy. In therapy the therapist speaks as the representative of the demands of reality, directly for the sake of the self-transformation of the patient, and indirectly for the sake of the therapist's own self-transformation, or at least self-confirmation. But speaking as the representative of reality is just what any teacher does. Thus education in general is just the fuller working out of the therapeutic project. What we normally call "therapy" is this project geared toward the self as a coherent center of consciousness and action—the self as an individualized body in the world. What we typically call "education" is this same project focused not on the specific individual in her or his unique specificity and singularity, but focused, rather, on the specifics of the demands of world of "others as such" to which this individual and all others must answer. What we typically call "education," then, takes over the project of therapy roughly from the point of view of the human implied in the narrative of civil society.

Education and Philosophy

We have been comparing the relationship of therapy with the notion of education, and we have noticed that the roles defined for therapist and patient pertain in truth to any teaching situation, inasmuch as what is ultimately at stake in therapy—self-knowledge through the endorsement of others—is what is ultimately at play in all teaching. Indeed, "objectivity" has now appeared as an immanent norm of intersubjective life, and thus therapy itself is an unfolding of the project of learning the truth about reality. The social institution of education is the institutional attempt to fulfill this project, and is thus inherently rooted in the human values that emerge in the therapeutic situation. Of course, this is typically not noticed either by students or teachers, and especially not by the makers of educational policy. On the contrary, education is typically treated as a matter of the simple transfer of information and the correlative development of useful skills. From the beginning of this study, we have been recognizing the problems in principle with the notion of information-transfer in experience: experience, on the contrary, is always interpretive, bodily, and rooted in projects of intersubjective confirmation. There is, however, a prevailing narrative of human identity at play in our culture—the narrative of civil society, which is the narrative of normalcy—and the model of education as information-transfer is of a piece with this narrative of human identity. Just as we have criticized the notion of the normal individual that is implied in the narrative of civil society, so too must we replace the notion of education as information transfer with the notion of education as therapeutic self-transcendence through respect for the demands of intersubjective reality. The institution of education is right in interpreting itself as representing the realm of universal truth: as we have seen all along, the nature of our bodily life is to be responding to the determinate demands of our world, and thus experience is not merely a matter of arbitrary imagination, but has as its own immanent norm the notion of disciplined study of the other on its own terms. The institution of education is wrong, however, to the extent that it treats this disciplinary reality as meaningful in independence of the bodily, emotional, intersubjective lives of persons negotiating their erotic relations with each other. As John Dewey puts it in *The Child and the Curriculum*, education must integrate the demands of the discipline with the needs of the child. Education properly understood is disciplinary study in the service of human maturation.

Indeed, with a little further reflection, we can see that, as was just intimated, what we have marked out in our discussion of the therapeutic relation are not the special roles that apply in psychiatrist's offices or in classrooms but are rather the roles of interpersonal life in general. *To be a person is always to act as the representative of otherness as such*, always to be carving an image, so to speak, of what it is to be human. This is just another way of saying what we established in chapter 4, namely, that our very nature is to be embedded in a project of self-confirmation that is inseparable from a project of supporting and being supported by the development of others whose identities cannot be separated from our own. What we have in fact seen is the demands of interpersonal respect as such, and we have seen this through looking at therapy simply because the therapeutic relation is the relationship in which the universal demands of human development are explicit. As we saw above, neurosis is a universal condition of human development, and therefore there is no one who is not intrinsically motivated toward the project of therapeutic self-transcendence. The issue is simply the extent to which one recognizes this and the extent to which this process is supported by the others who constitute our environment. Similarly, all education will always be about our intersubjective world, despite the way that this ultimate context remains latent when we reflect with great intensity on the minute details of our world, and despite the veneer of impersonality that comes with the scope and institutional realization of education. It is thus in therapy and education that we find our proper form, for these are the practices of self-transcendence within neurotic life, and this is just the description of our essential reality. Philosophy is the self-conscious taking up of this project.

By a consideration of the demands of personal experience, we have seen that therapy, as *intimate, interpersonal care*, is our natural fulfillment. By reflecting on the logic of the therapeutic relationship, we have seen that therapy finds its fulfillment in education and now, ultimately, we can say that philosophy, that is, phenomenology as a project of self-knowledge as self-transcendence is the completed form of education. Our reality is to be drawn to self-transcendence, and philosophy is the explicit recognition of our situation as calling us to resolve it through self-transformation. To be philosophical is to hear from the world the call, the imperative, that Rainer Maria Rilke hears in ancient art: "You must change your life!" Philosophy is heeding this call to grow. Indeed, this is philosophy understood in one of its earliest incarnations, namely, the investigations of Socrates. Socrates sought self-knowledge through questioning others about how they saw things, and through working with them to see if their views could cohere with each other and with themselves. Socrates defined his role as philosophical interlocutor as to speak on behalf of the one with whom he speaks, working out the implications, the latent commitments, that are constitutive of that other's views, teaching others to adopt the same practice. In Socratic philosophizing we thus have the model for the fulfillment of human life as it has been understood and articulated in this work.

What form does this philosophical practice take? To what is our self-transcendence directed? There is no answer to these questions. Our self-transformative actions must precisely take us beyond the boundaries and terms of our already established identities. Self-transformation must be a creative action launched from the tensions and fueled by the resources that constitute our embodied contact with the intersubjective world, an expression of a new identity. Philosophy is the self-conscious embrace of our erotic and linguistic character, the pursuit of caring engagements with others through creative self-expression and self-articulation.

The Human Situation

The story of Socrates may exemplify the ideal of dyadic interpersonal relations, but it also reminds us that such relations do not constitute the totality of the intersubjective world upon whose support we rely. Socrates himself was killed by the state because that social organization could not tolerate his challenge to familiarity and his questioning of the very nature of law and value. This reminds us that it is not simply up to our single selves to determine the kinds of activities in which we can engage, but that the structures of society in general set various limits to human development. We are social beings, so the question of therapy cannot fail to be a social and political question.

• We have already seen that the central issue we face in our social life is the image of ourselves that our social group will endorse. This issue must be the central theme of the analysis of political relations: we must ask what portrait of human life a society explicitly projects in its explicit laws and narratives and what portrait of human life it implicitly or behaviorally projects through the specific forms of human interaction that it tolerates, supports, opposes, and so forth. We have already studied the issue of the goal of social life in general in chapter 4. We must look at this issue of a society's implicit and explicit portraiture of human life in the context of the logic and goals of society that we earlier articulated.

We saw in chapter 4 that the ultimate goal of social life must be to challenge the primacy of familiarity in the context of allowing the development of free human individuals in a society of universal equality as that notion has been understood in the context of our bodily intersubjectivity. In general, however, we do not live in societies that take such a form. Consequently, our lives are normally shaped by social situations that introduce problems into our projects of self-development.

• We have already seen that we are born into societies that already operate according to principles, the intelligibility of which is not something to which we are privy. Societies act according to various implicit traditions and explicit rules, and it is by embracing the vision expressed by these principles that we make ourselves individuals capable of being recognized by others as legitimate members of their society. Our most basic habituations are those by which we become accustomed to acting automatically in accordance with the organizing principles of our societies, whether the immediate familial society or the larger culture. For us, these principles *fundamentally* function as ways by which we establish a sense of ourselves. Before anything else, then, *for the individual* society and its principles of order exists as a thesis about self-identity: the governing significance of any social order is how it names, how it identifies its members, what it calls them. Our analysis has shown that our fundamental struggle is one of searching for an identity, and we see that society itself acts as the phenomenon of intersubjectivity that calls us to this struggle *and also* a determinate contender within this struggle that endorses and enforces a specific claim about who we are. It is in this sense that social forms are inseparable from personal development.

We have also seen, however, that social groups can be organized around different principles for interpreting the identities of their members. Families assert the primacy of familiarity, and demand that we find ourselves within the familiar patterns of family life. The society of normal civic values is precisely a critique of the society of family values, for the value of normalcy is a challenge to the legitimacy of the value of familiarity as such. We have seen further the need for a society built on the value of free singular selves who recognize the inescapability of embodiment and familiarity, and this society, while it is by no means a reversion to family values, is precisely a critique of the society of the stoic value of normalcy. The society of stoic values, then, is not society *simpliciter* but is one essential species of society, which itself takes a place in the developmental pattern of social life according (as we have seen in chapter 4) to the demands that social life itself places upon itself.

This society of normal, stoic values, however, is by no means an insignificant species of social life. Like the family, the society of stoic values is a standard social space in which most of us—those of us in the West, at least—live. We all have a family life (or its equivalent) and all of us who have grown past that (though still having neurotic ties to it) likewise have an experience of stoic civil life. It is precisely our day-to-day participation in a society that says, "we are all free individuals who can choose for ourselves and who are separate from others, from things in the world and from our bodies" that is this experience. Indeed, this book began with the recognition that it is this society that provides for most of us most of the time that which we consider to be our real home: when we ask ourselves who we are we normally think of ourselves as normal, civilized individuals, as stoics. This society of these values is very much the society of modern Europe and the United Sates to be sure, and to differing degrees characterizes society in the rest of the industrialized world. It is the society of modern industrial capitalism, the society that advocates competitive individualism in business and politics.

Indeed, this individualist society is the society built around the denial that human freedom and self-identity is an achievement. It denies that there are social and material conditions that are necessary for mental health. It is a society built around a definition of the human individual that simultaneously justifies the practices of the society and undercuts the possibility for the proper development and flourishing of the individuals who make up that society. It is this modern capitalist society that exemplifies Freud's description, in *Civilization and Its Discontents*, of a society that furthers itself by crippling the mental health of its members. Indeed, in its most extreme form, the social cultivation of stoic values is the production of an antihuman, warrior society, whether ancient Sparta or German society of the 1930s and 1940s. Mental health is a most personal issue, but it is an issue that cannot be addressed outside the context of social life. The stoic ideal of normalcy and liberal equality is indeed our liberation from the slavery of family values, but the greatest threat to the human development of mental health within extrafamilial social life is this very same stoic ideal.

Bibliography

Ackerman, Nathan W. *The Psychodynamics of Family Life*. (New York: Basic, 1958).

Aeschylus, *Oresteia*, translated and introduced by Richmond Lattimore. (Chicago: University of Chicago Press, 1953).

Althusser, Louis. *The Future Lasts a Long Time*, translated by Richard Veasey. (London: Chatto and Windus, 1993).

Aristotle. *The Complete Works of Aristotle*, 2 Vols., edited by Jonathan Barnes. (Princeton: Princeton University Press, 1984).

———. *De Anima*. Greek text with facing English translated by W. S. Hett, Vol. 288 of the Loeb Classical Library. Rev. ed. (Cambridge: Harvard University Press, 1957).

———. *Ethica Nicomachea*, edited by L. Bywater. (Oxford: Clarendon Press, 1894).

———. *Parts of Animals, Movement of Animals, Progression of Animals*. Rev. ed. Greek text with facing English translated by A. L. Peck and E. S. Forster, Vol. 323 of the Loeb Classical Library. (Cambridge: Harvard University Press, 1961).

———. *Politics*. Greek text with facing English translated by H. Rackman, Loeb Classical Library. (Cambridge: Harvard University Press, 1950).

Bateson, Gregory. *Steps to an Ecology of Mind* (Chicago: University of Chicago Press, 2000).

———. "A Social Scientist Views the Emotions," in P. Knapp (ed.). *Expression of the Emotions in Man*. (Madison, Wis.: International University Press, 1963).

———, and J. Ruesch, *Communication: The Social Matrix of Psychiatry*. (New York: Norton, 1951).

Bergson, Henri. *Matter and Memory*, translated by Nancy Margaret Paul and W. Scott Palmer. (New York: Humanities Press, 1978).

———. *Time and Free Will*. (Montana: Kessinger Publishing, N.D.).

Berne, Eric. *Games People Play*. (New York: Grove, 1964).

Binswanger, Ludwig. *Being-in-the-World*, translated by Jacob Needleman. (New York: Harper, 1967).

Bollas, Christopher. *The Mystery of Things*. (New York: Routledge, 1999).

———. *The Shadow of the Object: Psychoanalysis of the Unthought Known*. (New York: Columbia University Press, 1987).

Bourdieu, Pierre. *The Logic of Practice*. (Stanford: Stanford University Press, 1990).

Brenner, Ira. *Dissociation of Trauma: Theory, Phenomenology and Technique*. (Madison, Wis.: International Universities Press, 2001).

Bullard, Dexter M. (ed.). *Psychoanalysis and Psychotherapy: Selected Papers of Frieda Fromm-Reichmann*. (Chicago: University of Chicago Press, 1959).

Bullowa, M. (ed). *Before Speech: The Beginnings of Human Communication*. (Cambridge: Cambridge University Press, 1979).

Burton, Arthur, and Robert E. Harris. *Clinical Studies of Personality*. (New York: Harper, 1955).

Casey, Edward S. *Getting Back into Place: Toward a Renewed Understanding of the Place-World*. (Bloomington: Indiana University Press, 1993).

Collingwood, R. G. *The Principles of Art*. (Oxford: Clarendon Press, 1938).

———. *Speculum Mentis*. (Oxford: Clarendon Press, 1924).

de Beauvoir, Simone. *The Ethics of Ambiguity*, translated by Bernard Frechtman. (New York: Citadel Press, 1991).

———. *The Second Sex*, translated by H. M. Parshley. (New York: Knopf, 1971).

Deleuze Gilles, and Félix Guattari. *L'Anti-Oedipe*. (Paris: Editions de Minuit, 1972), translated by Robert Hurley, Mark Seem, and Helen R. Lane as *Anti-Oedipus: Capitalism and Schizophrenia*. (New York: Viking, 1977).

Descartes, René. *Discourse on Method and Meditations on First Philosophy*, 4th ed., translated by Donald A. Cress. (Indianapolis: Hackett, 1998).

Dewey, John. *How We Think*. (Boston: Heath, 1910).

———. *The School and Society* and *The Child and the Curriculum*. (Chicago: University of Chicago Press, 1990).

Eisenstein, Victor W. (ed.). *Neurotic Interaction in Marriage*. (New York: Basic, 1956).

Faulkner, William. *The Unvanquished*. (New York: Random, 1965).

———. *The Sound and the Fury*. (New York: Random House, 1990).

Fenichel, Otto. *The Psychoanalytic Theory of Neurosis.* (New York: Norton, 1945).

Fichte, Johann Gottlieb. *Grundlage der gesammten Wissenschaftslehre* in *Fichtes Werke, Band 1, zur theoretischen Philosophie I*, hrsg. v. I. H. Fichte. (Berlin: Walter de Gruyter and Co., 1971), translated by Peter Heath and John Lachs as *The Science of Knowledge.* (Cambridge: Cambridge University Press, 1982).

———. *Grundlage des Naturrechts nach Principien der Wissenschaftslehre*, in *Sammtliche Werke zweite Abteilung, a. zur Rechts—und Sittenlehre*, hrsg. v. J. H. Fichte. (Berlin: Verlag von Zeit und Comp., 1845), translated by A. E. Kroeger as *The Science of Rights.* (London: Routledge and Kegan Paul, 1889).

Freud, Sigmund. *An Outline of Psychoanalysis*, translated by James Strachey. (New York: Norton, 1949).

———. *Beyond the Pleasure Principle*, translated by James Strachey. (New York: Norton, 1961).

———. *Civilization and Its Discontents*, translated by James Strachey. (New York: Norton, 1961).

———. *On Psychopathology*, Vol. 10 of the Pelican Freud Library, translated by James Strachey. (Harmondsworth: Penguin, 1979).

———. *Therapy and Technique*, edited by Philip Rieff. (New York: Macmillan, 1963).

———. *Three Essays on the Theory of Sexuality*, translated by James Strachey. (New York: Harper, 1975).

Gibson, James J. *The Ecological Approach to Visual Perception.* (Hillsdale N.J.: Erlbaum, 1986).

Gopnik, Alison, Andrew N. Meltzoff, and Patricia K. Kuhl. *The Scientist in the Crib: Minds, Brains and How Children Learn.* (New York: Morrow, 1999).

Grinker, Roy R., and Fred P. Robbins. *Psychosomatic Case Book.* (New York: Blakiston Company, 1954).

Gustafson, James P. *The Complex Secret of Brief Psychotherapy.* (New York: Norton, 1986).

Halbwachs, Maurice. *On Collective Memory*, translated by Lewis A. Coser. (Chicago: University of Chicago Press, 1992).

Hegel, G. W. F. *Grundlinien der Philosophie des Rechts.* 4. Auflage, hrsg. v. Johannes Hoffmeister. (Hamburg: Felix Meiner Verlag, 1955), translated by T. M. Knox as *Philosophy of Right.* (Oxford: Oxford University Press, 1967 [paperback]).

Hegel, G. W. F. *Phänomenologie des Geistes*. Hrsg. v. Hans-Friedrich Wessels und Heinrich Clairmont. (Hamburg: Felix Meiner Verlag, 1988), translated by A. V. Miller as *Phenomenology of Spirit*. (Oxford: Oxford University Press, 1977).

————. *Philosophy of Spirit*, translated by A. V. Miller. (Oxford: Oxford University Press, 1970).

Heidegger, Martin. *Basic Writings*, 2nd ed., edited by David Farrell Krell. (New York: Harper, 1992).

————. *Sein und Zeit*, 5. Auflage. (Tübingen, Germany: Max Niemeyer, 1941), translated by Joan Stambaugh as *Being and Time*. (Albany: State University of New York Press, 1996).

Husserl, Edmund. *Cartesianische Meditationen*. (Hamburg: Felix Meiner, 1987), translated by Dorion Cairns as *Cartesian Meditations*. (The Hague: Martinus Nijhoff, 1960).

James, William. *The Principles of Psychology*, 2 Vols. (New York: Henry Holt, 1890).

Johnson, Mark. *The Body in the Mind: The Bodily Basis of Meaning, Imagination, and Reason*. (Chicago: University of Chicago Press, 1987).

Joyce, James. *Ullyses*. (Harmondsworth, England: Penguin, 1960).

Kant, Immanuel. *Critique of Pure Reason*, translated by Norman Kemp Smith. (New York: St. Martin's, 1929).

Karen, Robert. *Becoming Attached: First Relationships and How They Shape Our Capacity to Love*. (Oxford: Oxford University Press, 1998).

Klein, Melanie. *The Selected Melanie Klein*. (Harmondsworth: Penguin, 1986).

Köhler, Wolfgang. *Dynamics in Psychology*. (New York: Liveright, 1940).

Kraines, Samuel Henry. *The Therapy of the Neuroses and Psychoses: A Sociopsychobiologic Analysis and Resynthesis*, 2nd ed. (Philadelphia: Lea and Febiger, 1943).

Kristeva, Julia. *La révolution du langage poétique*. (Paris: Éditions du Seuil, 1974), translated by Margaret Walker as *Revolution in Poetic Language*. (New York: Columbia University Press, 1984).

Lacan, Jacques. *Écrits*. (Paris: Éditions du Seuil, 1966), selections translated by Alan Sheridan as *Écrits: A Selection*. (New York: Norton, 1977).

————. *Le Séminaire de Jacques Lacan. Livre 1*. (Paris: Éditions du Seuil, 1975), translated by John Forrester as *The Seminar of Jacques Lacan. Book 1, Freud's Papers on Technique, 1953–1954*. (New York: Norton, 1991).

Lacan, Jacques. *Le Séminaire de Jacques Lacan. Livre 11*, "*Les quatre concepts fondamentaux de la psychanalyse.*" (Paris: Éditions du Seuil, 1973), translated by Alan Sheridan as *The Seminar of Jacques Lacan. Book 11, The Four Fundamental Concepts of Psychoanalysis.* (New York: Norton, 1981).

Laing, R. D. *The Divided Self.* (London: Penguin, 1990).

———. *The Politics of the Family.* (Toronto: Canadian Broadcasting Company, 1969).

———. *Sanity, Madness and the Family.* (Harmondsworth: Penguin, 1970).

———. *Self and Others.* (London: Penguin, 1969).

Lampert, Jay. *Synthesis and Backwards Reference in Husserl's Logical Investigations.* (Dordrecht, Netherlands: Kluwer, 1995).

Leder, Drew. *The Absent Body.* (Chicago: University of Chicago Press, 1990).

Lidz, Theodore, and Stephen Fleck. *Schizophrenia and the Family*, 2nd ed. (New York: International Universities Press, 1985).

Lingis, Alphonso. *Excesses: Eros and Culture.* (Albany: State University of New York Press, 1983).

Marx, Karl, and Friedrich Engels. *Selected Works*, 3 Vols. (Moscow: Progress Publishers, 1969).

Maturana, Humberto R., and Francisco J. Varela. *Autopoiesis and Cognition: The Realization of the Living.* Boston Studies in the Philosophy of Science, no. 42. (Dordrecht, Netherlands: D. Reidel Publishing Company, 1980).

McDowell, John. *Mind and World.* (Cambridge: Harvard University Press, 1994).

Merleau-Ponty, Maurice. *Consciousness and the Acquisition of Language*, translated by Hugh J. Silverman. (Evanston, Chicago: Northwestern University Press, 1973).

———. *La Phénoménologie de la Perception.* (Paris: Éditions Gallimard, 1945), translated into English by Colin Smith as *Phenomenology of Perception.* (London: Routledge and Kegan Paul, 1962).

———. *In Praise of Philosophy and Other Essays*, translated by John Wild, James Edie, and John O'Neill. (Evanston, Chicago: Northwestern University Press, 1963).

———. *The Primacy of Perception*, edited by James Edie. (Evanston, Chicago: Northwestern University Press, 1964).

———. *Signs*, translated by Richard C. McCleary. (Evanston, Chicago: Northwestern University Press, 1962).

Merleau-Ponty, Maurice. *La Structure du Comportement*. (Paris: Presses Universitaires de France, 1942), translated into English by Alden L. Fisher as *The Structure of Behavior*. (Boston: Beacon, 1959).

Minuchin, Salvador, and H. Charles Fishman. *Family Therapy Techniques*. (Cambridge, MA.: Harvard University Press, 1981).

Morris, David. The Sense of Space. Ph.D. diss., University of Toronto, 1995.

Morris, David. "Touching Intelligence." *Journal of the Philosophy of Sport* 39 (2002):149–162.

Minuchin, Salvador, and H. Charles Fishman. *Family Therapy Techniques*. (Cambridge, MA.: Harvard University Press, 1981).

Napier, Augustus Y., and Carl A. Whitaker. *The Family Crucible*. (New York: Harper Perennial, 1988).

Nietzsche, Friedrich. *Beyond Good and Evil: Prelude to a Philosophy of the Future*, translated by Walter Kaufmann. (New York: Vintage Books, 1966).

———. *On the Genealogy of Morals*, translated by Walter Kaufmann and R. J. Hollingdale. (New York: Vintage Books, 1989).

O'Connor, Kevin J. *The Play Therapy Primer*, 2nd ed. (New York: Wiley, 2000).

Piaget, Jean. *The Origin of Intelligence in Children*, translated by Margaret Cook. (New York: International Universities Press, 1952).

Plato. "Apologia Socratis," in *Opera* I, edited by John Burnet. (Oxford: Clarendon Press, 1900).

———. *The Collected Dialogues of Plato*, edited by Edith Hamilton and Huntingdon Cairns. (Princeton: Princeton University Press, 1961).

———. "Gorgias," in *Opera* III, edited by John Burnet. (Oxford: Clarendon Press, 1903).

———. "Symposium," in *Opera* II, edited by John Burnet. (Oxford: Clarendon Press, 1901).

Proclus. *The Elements of Theology*, translated by E. R. Dodds. (Oxford: Clarendon Press, 1963).

Proust, Marcel. *Swann's Way*, translated by C. K. Scott Moncrieff. (London: Chatto and Windus, 1969–1970).

Rivera, Margo (ed.). *Fragment by Fragment: Feminist Perspectives on Memory and Child Sexual Abuse*. (Charlottetown, Canada: Gynergy Books, 1999).

Rochat, P. (ed.). *The Self in Early Infancy*. (New York: North-Holland-Elsevier Science Publishers, 1995).

Russon, John. *The Self and Its Body in Hegel's Phenomenology of Spirit*. (Toronto: University of Toronto Press, 1997).

———. "Aristotle's Animative Epistemology." *Idealistic Studies* 25 (1995):241–253.

———. "Embodiment and Responsibility: Merleau-Ponty and the Ontology of Nature." *Man and World* 27 (1994):291–308.

———. "Eros and Education: Plato's Transformative Epistemology." *Laval Théologique et Philosophique* 56 (2000):113–125.

———. "Heidegger, Hegel and Ethnicity: The Ritual Basis of Self-Identity." *Southern Journal of Philosophy* 33 (1995):509–532.

———. "The Bodily Unconscious in Freud's *Three Essays*." In Jon Mills (ed), *Rereading Freud: Psychoanalysis Through Philosophy*. (Albany: State University of New York Press, forthcoming).

Ryle, Gilbert. *The Concept of Mind*. (New York: Harper, 1949).

Sartre, Jean-Paul. *L'Être et le Néant: Essai d'ontologie phénoménologique*. (Paris: Gallimard, 1943), translated by Hazel E. Barnes as *Being and Nothingness*. (New York: Philosophical Library, 1956).

———. *L'Existentialisme est un humanisme*. (Paris: Éditions Nagel, 1946), translated by Philip Mairet as *Existentialism and Humanism*. (London: Eyre Methuen, 1973 [paperback]).

———. *La Nausée*. (Paris: Gallimard, 1938), translated by Robert Bladdick as *Nausea*. (London, England: Penguin, 2001).

Sellars, Wilfrid. "Empiricism and the Philosophy of Mind." *Minnesota Studies in the Philosophy of Science* 1 (1956):253–329.

Shakespeare, William. *Romeo and Juliet*, edited by T. J. B. Spencer. (Harmondsworth: Penguin, 1967).

Sheets-Johnstone, Maxine. *The Primacy of Movement*. (Philadelphia: John Benjamins, 1999).

Simion, Francesca, and George Butterworth (eds). *The Development of Sensory, Motor and Cognitive Capacities in Early Infancy: From Perception to Cognition*. (East Sussex: The Psychology Press, 1998).

Sophocles. *The Theban Plays*, translated by E. F. Watling. (New York: Penguin, 1947).

———. *Sophocles II*, edited by David Grene and Richmond Lattimore. (Chicago: University of Chicago Press, 1969).

Sparshott, Francis. *Taking Life Seriously: A Study of the Argument of the Nicomachean Ethics*. (Toronto: University of Toronto Press, 1994).

Stern, Daniel N. *The Interpersonal World of the Infant: A View from Psychoanalysis and Developmental Psychology*. (New York: Basic, 1985).

Sullivan, Harry Stack. *The Interpersonal Theory of Psychiatry*. (New York: Norton, 1953).

———. *The Psychiatric Interview*. (New York: Norton, 1970).

———. *Schizophrenia as a Human Process*. (New York: Norton, 1962).

Talero, Maria. "The Temporal Context of Freedom in Merleau-Ponty's *Phenomenology of Perception*." Ph.D. diss., Pennsylvania State University, 2002.

Thewelheit, Klaus. *Male Fantasies*, 2 Vols., translated by Stephen Conway, Erica Carter, and Chris Turner. (Minneapolis: University of Minnesota Press, 1987 [Vol. 1] and 1989 [Vol. 2]).

Thompson, Jack George. *The Psychobiology of the Emotions*. (New York: Plenum Press, 1988).

Varela, Francisco, Evan Thompson, and Eleanor Rosch. *The Embodied Mind*. (Cambridge: Massachusetts Institute of Technology Press, 1991).

Weber, Max. *Die Protestantische Ethik und der Geist des Kapitalismus*. (Tübingen, Germany: Mohr, 1934), translated into English by Talcott Parsons as *The Protestant Ethic and the Spirit of Capitalism*. (New York: Scribner, 1958).

Winnicott, D. W. *The Child, the Family and the Outside World* (Harmondsworth: Penguin, 1968).

Index